SNARLING
TIGER,
DIRTY RAT

SNARLING TIGER, DIRTY RAT

Stella Hyde

Illustrated by
Tonwen Jones

P

Perigee

THE BERKLEY PUBLISHING GROUP
Published by the Penguin Group
Penguin Group (USA) Inc.
375 Hudson Street, New York,
New York 10014, USA
Penguin Group (Canada), 90 Eglinton Avenue
East, Suite 700, Toronto, Ontario M4P 2Y3, Canada
(a division of Pearson Penguin Canada Inc.)
Penguin Books Ltd., 80 Strand,
London WC2R 0RL, England
Penguin Group Ireland, 25 St. Stephen's Green,
Dublin 2, Ireland (a division of Penguin Books Ltd.)
Penguin Group (Australia), 250 Camberwell Road,
Camberwell, Victoria 3124, Australia
(a division of Pearson Australia Group Pty. Ltd.)
Penguin Books India Pvt. Ltd., 11 Community
Centre, Panchsheel Park, New Delhi—110 017, India
Penguin Group (NZ), cnr. Airborne and Rosedale
Roads, Albany, Auckland 1310, New Zealand
(a division of Pearson New Zealand Ltd.)
Penguin Books (South Africa) (Pty.) Ltd.,
24 Sturdee Avenue, Rosebank, Johannesburg
2196, South Africa

Penguin Books Ltd., Registered Offices: 80 Strand,
London WC2R 0RL, England

PRINTING HISTORY
Perigee trade paperback edition / February 2006

PERIGEE is a registered trademark of
Penguin Group (USA) Inc.
The "P" design is a trademark belonging to
Penguin Group (USA) Inc.

Printed in China
10 9 8 7 6 5 4 3 2 1

International Standard Book Number
0-399-53248-X

This book has been cataloged by
the Library of Congress

This book was conceived, designed,
and produced by

THE IVY PRESS LIMITED
The Old Candlemakers
West Street, Lewes
East Sussex, BN7 2NZ, UK

Creative Director Peter Bridgewater
Publisher Jason Hook
Art Director Karl Shanahan
Designer Tonwen Jones
Illustrator Tonwen Jones
Project Editor Mandy Greenfield

CONTENTS

INTRODUCTION

You all know your sun sign, right? The zodiac influence that makes you behave badly and explains all your unsavory habits? Did you know there is another influence you can blame? Well, there is, according to the ancient philosophies of China, Vietnam, Korea, and Japan. In the Eastern tradition, a beast lurks in your heart, giving you another great excuse to give in to unacceptable activities. In fact, the only thing most Westerners know about Chinese astrology is the procession of animals; it's based on the Moon, Jupiter, and the Pole Star, because Asia faces the heavens at a slightly different angle from the Middle East, where Western stargazing was invented. So this book will stick with what you know.

The animals follow each other around in a perpetual 12-year cycle, starting with the Rat and ending with the Pig, then starting again and continuing to infinity, like tigers pacing in a zoo. As long as you know the year of your birth, you can find your inner beast. "Fair enough," you say. "Jung gave us our animus/anima, why not have an animal companion along as well?" Yes, but have you considered what a mess most animals generate? I will tell you, because there is more than enough material emphasizing the brave, noble, furry, feathery, and adorable aspects of your companion animal. We are going to concentrate on the messy, inconvenient, smelly, and dangerous aspects. If you think all the Supreme Being's creatures are sacred and innocent, or you're feeling a bit fragile or sorry for yourself, look away now, because there will be no punch-pulling.

Although even the most comatose among you are able to find which animal rules your year (all you need to know is your birthday), it is of course not that simple. You will have to know a bit about the five elements of Eastern philosophy, and the energy-balancing act of yin and yang. This introductory section also explains the animal husbandry that allows you a couple of additional beasts, lower down the pecking order. Then, in the main part of the book, we go through every animal in detail, examining its temperament, mating habits, daily routine, habitat, and place in the food chain. Of course, yours won't be anything like the cuddly pet that nestles behind your rib cage, but you will be amazed at how accurate it is about your friends and family!

So, here is the whole zoo: red in tooth, claw, and beak, reviewed from a position of safety behind a whip and a chair. It won't tame the beast in you, but you'll find out where that howling at night is coming from.

THE BEAST IN YOU

Twelve animals grunt and howl their way around the Eastern zodiac. They are, in order: Rat, Ox, Tiger, Rabbit, Dragon, Snake, Horse, Sheep, Monkey, Rooster, Dog, and Pig, an eclectic menagerie of domestic, farmyard, wild, and feral, with a shot of fantasy (Dragon) thrown in.

You get three goes at choosing a lifelong animal companion: you have your year animal, your month animal, and your hour animal. Sometimes this combination comes out all harmonious (agreeable trio of Pig, Sheep, and Rabbit, for instance) or exotic (Tiger, Dragon, and Monkey); but mostly, as this is the darkside, it results in three incompatible animals trapped in a sack, spitting fur, feathers, and scales. Worse still, you could get the same animal each time. If you were born in December 1972 at midnight, you'd be a Triple Rat ... It doesn't bear thinking about, does it?

How Did It Come to This?

Why no sloths? Why no bottom feeders? Why no cockroaches? In short, why no animals that would express our inner beasts rather better? This is all down to Buddha. According to many Chinese and Vietnamese sources, the story is that when Buddha was about to finally step off the tedious cycle of being and leave the planet, he called all the animals in the world to come and say good-bye to him. It was New Year's Day and he was going to have a farewell party. Disappointingly, only this bunch turned up. To get to Buddha, they had to swim across a river to him, and this is the order in which they reached him. In gratitude he named a year after each of them, starting with the Rat, who stepped ashore first—but only because he had bummed a lift on the Ox.

If you pay attention, you will notice that a few of the animals creep in using different names. The Pig is sometimes called the Boar, as if that makes you sound more of a contender; the Ox is sometimes known as the Buffalo, but that's just cultural semantics; the Rooster is called the Hen or Chicken, but that's just dimorphism; the Sheep is sometimes called the Ram (*see Boar above*), but also the Goat. In the West, this is a whole other animal, a lot madder and hotter and more unpredictable, so when you are baa-ing your way through the Sheep chapter (*see pages 130–145*) and feel you have been sold a bit short, consider a career change to Goat. The greatest divergence comes with the Rabbit: also known, especially in Vietnam, as the Cat. Now call me old-fashioned, but Cats and Rabbits are completely different animals. There is, inevitably, a story that explains this; read it in the panel to the left.

CAT OR RABBIT?

When Buddha was sending out the invitations to his party, he asked Rat (nosy, mobile, inveterate gossip) to spread the word and encourage the other animals to ask their friends. Rat told his best friend, the Cat (yes, I know, but wait). Cat was thrilled, and so anxious to go to the party that he asked Rat to wake him up in good time. Rat "forgot." Next day, when Rat realized they were a man short and that Buddha might have something to say about it, he quickly invited the first animal he saw, which happened to be Rabbit. So Cat slept in, Cat missed the party, and now Cat hunts rats and mice mercilessly. In Vietnam, they still call the Rabbit the Cat—possibly just to annoy Rat.

FINDING YOUR BEAST

It's not rocket science working out which animal lurks under your rib cage; all you have to know is what year you were born in. It gets a bit tricksy if you were a January or February baby. This is because the Eastern year follows the Moon's wanderings rather than the Sun's, and consequently the New Year does not start on a fixed date.

Each lunar month lasts 29½ days; an extra month is slipped in every two and a half years to make the math work (don't ask!). You do not need to understand the details—the important thing is that it means the year can start anywhere between mid-January and late February. For example, 1974 is the Year of the Tiger; but being born in 1974 doesn't automatically mean you are a big Snarling Cat—if your birthday is before 23 January, you are a Plodding Ox. It also means that anyone born up to 10 February 1975 is not the dear little Rabbit everyone thinks they are.

We have made it easy for you with the year charts at the back of the book (*see pages 218–221*); if you are January- or February-born, just make sure that you pay attention.

Animal of the Month

As well as a whole year, each animal looks after a month of its own. In the Chinese lunar calendar, these "months" were agricultural seasons, but they slot well into the Western arrangement. For instance, Rat's season (called "Little Snow and Great Snow") fills the tail end of November and most of December, so it slots well into the month of December and the Western zodiac sign of Sagittarius (*see pages 210–217 for more about this*).

MONTH	ANIMAL	SUN SIGN	MONTH	ANIMAL	SUN SIGN
January	Ox	Capricorn	July	Sheep	Cancer
February	Tiger	Aquarius	August	Monkey	Leo
March	Rabbit	Pisces	September	Rooster	Virgo
April	Dragon	Aries	October	Dog	Libra
May	Snake	Taurus	November	Pig	Scorpio
June	Horse	Gemini	December	Rat	Sagittarius

Animal of the Hour

And guess what: each animal has another little job on the side, looking after the hour of your birth. For zodiacal purposes (and 24-hour party people), the Chinese day starts at 11:00 p.m. It is divided into 12 two-hour slots, and each one has its own animal—starting with the Rat, as usual (*see page 13 for further information*).

ZOO TIME

Although you are legally entitled to three animals (year, hour, month) in the menagerie of your heart, in Chinese tradition the hour animal is second in the pack order. Sadly, for those of you longing for something a little more refined—a cheetah, perhaps, or a gyrfalcon—hour animals are the usual suspects, double shifting, trapped in a minicycle, like a hamster wheel within a wheel.

As we have seen, the Chinese system divides the day into 12 two-hour blocks, and each animal rules a block, beginning with the Rat.

So, if the animal in your heart seems a little too tame/wild/ scary for your profile, check out who is on the loose when you first appeared in this vale of tears. Of course, you can only know which other animal companion you are entitled to if you know the actual hour of your birth, but you will have to find that out for yourself—I am not your mom! It's much the same as the ascendant sign in Western astrology, although much easier to work out. See the Companion Animals pages in each chapter for a gloomier résumé.

The Hours

Hour of the Rat 11:00 p.m.–12:59 a.m.
The graveyard shift, which suits your average Rat just fine, because no one can see you raiding the garbage cans.

Hour of the Ox 1:00–2:59 a.m.
According to old stockmen's tales, this is the time when the cattle wake up and discuss fat stock prices and dairy futures quietly among themselves.

Hour of the Tiger 3:00–4:59 a.m.
This is the darkest hour before dawn, but it suits you because you have giant, all-available-light-collecting cat's eyes.

Hour of the Rabbit 5:00–6:59 a.m.
You put it about that you have no conception of this time of day, but this is when you get up so that you can get ahead of the opposition without apparent effort.

Hour of the Dragon 7:00–8:59 a.m.
Exactly the right time to seize the day and show who's boss, but not so early that ignorant people mistake you for the office cleaner.

Hour of the Snake 9:00–10:59 a.m.
The time for power breakfasting, fierce black coffee, and scheming your next takeover without getting out of bed.

Hour of the Horse 11:00 a.m.–12:59 p.m.
According to science, this is the the most productive time of the day, and you use it to gallop as far as you can before losing interest.

Hour of the Sheep 1:00–2:59 p.m.
Lunchtime! Two hours of indulgent munching in someone else's lush field and at someone else's expense.

Hour of the Monkey 3:00–4:59 p.m.
Crime stats indicate that this is the optimum time for opportunist housebreaking; everyone else loses focus as they approach the four o'clock sugar dip.

Hour of the Rooster 5:00–6:59 p.m.
Happy hour: early evening drinks parties, with you as guest of honor in your finest feathers. All over by seven, for you have a very early start.

Hour of the Dog 7:00–8:59 p.m.
Winding down after a long shift, with plenty of time to worry properly about all the things that went wrong.

Hour of the Pig 9:00–10:59 p.m.
Relax—agreeable hours lolling in front of the TV with a margarita in one trotter and a tub of Rocky Road ice cream in the other.

ELEMENTS AND ENERGIES

The elements loom large in every branch of Chinese philosophy, so don't expect them to duck out of a starring role in astrology. We have them in the West as well, but it is not the same. For a start, in the East there are five of them: Metal, Wood, Earth, Water, and Fire. In the West we have just four (Water, Fire, Earth, Air), replacing Metal and Wood with Air, but the idea is similar.

The five elements are forever locked in a kind of dance, and the idea is to spend your life trying to bring them into perfect harmony by adjustments to your environment or attitude. When all the elements are in balance, energy (chi) can flow healthily. That's what feng shui is all about. But naturally it is not as simple as shunting the furniture around and putting plants in unlikely places. You have to find out first what elemental baggage you are carrying.

Elementary Beasts

Each animal comes with a fixed element (*see opposite*). But each year also has its own element (*see pages 218–221*). And because two sorts of energy create the universe (yin and yang), each element has two ways of expressing itself. When the five-element and two-energy cycle is merged with the 12-animal year cycle, it produces the master 60-year cycle. Work with me here! Each of the five elements appears first as yang and then as yin, giving a 10-year cycle. To catch up with the 12-year animal cycle, both have to run for five sequences. In the course of the 60 years, each animal appears in each elemental year. So, for example, there are five Rat years in the course of the 60-year cycle, and in each one the Rat expresses its essential rattiness in a different way, depending on the year element. When your fixed element coincides with the year element of your birth, you are a pure Rat (or whatever); if you are a Rat (fixed element: Water) born in a Rat year ruled by Water (e.g. 1972), you are a maximum Rat; and if you are already a Triple Rat (*see page 8*), you are maximum Rat, supersized.

YIN AND YANG

What of yin and yang? The charts at the end of the book (*see pages 218–221*) and the start of each chapter tell you what kind of energy fires up your beast: either yin or yang. In Chinese philosophy, maintaining the perfect balance between yang and yin is the main task of the cosmos, so you can't opt out. Yang and yin energies throb through the zodiac like one of those post-party headaches you wish you didn't still get. Yang is positive, masculine, executive energy; Yang animals are Rat, Tiger, Dragon, Horse, Monkey, and Dog. Yin is negative, feminine, passive energy; yin animals are Ox, Rabbit, Snake, Sheep, Rooster, and Pig. Not much of a choice, is it?

Fixed Elements

Below are the animals grouped by their fixed elements. Smart readers will note that no animal has Earth as a fixed element. Most traditions maintain Earth is symbolically composed of the other four elements, so can't be allocated to an animal. A few obstinate astrologers feel that Ox, Dragon, Sheep, and Dog should have Earth as their fixed element, but they are rare.

Element	Animals
Metal	Monkey, Rooster, Dog
Wood	Tiger, Rabbit, Dragon
Water	Pig, Rat, Ox
Fire	Snake, Horse, Sheep

Special Note on the Fire Horse

Unlike any other animal in the Chinese zodiac, the Fire Horse (1906, 1966, but no worries now until 2026) is feared as a beast that consumes all in its path and wreaks havoc and devastation wherever it gallops. Review your 1966-born friends, and maybe get extra insurance. The lady Fire Horse is reputed to be even more deadly (wouldn't you know it). Apparently, Fire stallions can sometimes turn the inner demon into fame and glory on the field of sport or battle—if they don't self-combust first.

Know Your Elements

Each element expresses a different kind of energy, but they are all interlinked. In the Chinese tradition they can be arranged in a productive, cooperative, helpful (brightside) cycle or in a destructive, divisive, harmful (darkside) cycle. Guess which pattern we are going for?

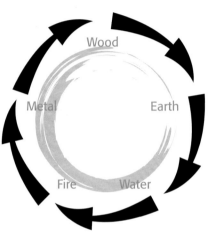

Wheel of Loathing

The animals that directly face each other on the wheel of the year loathe each other. This is because two identical energies meeting head-on repel each other, just as magnets with the same polarity repel one another. You know how it is when you meet someone who has all the same annoying flaws, tiresome tricks, and tedious mannerisms that you won't admit in yourself. Check the wheel for your *bête noire*.

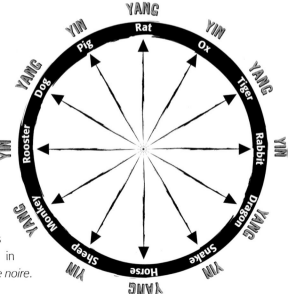

UNDESIRABLE ELEMENTS

Here are brief biogs of the five elements, showing you the worst it could get. Be comforted by the thought that your birth element will be restrained by other power-crazed elements loyal to your year of birth, hour animal, and month animal.

Metal

Metal energy is rigid, intense, and fast-moving and is all about attainment and accumulation (sometimes it's called Gold rather than Metal). It's ruled by Venus, which in the West is the planet of having it all—and then some. Metal-energy people want it all, and will get it, by the sword if they have to; they are inflexible and self-reliant, but very magnetic.

Wood

Wood energy is about expansion, progress, grandeur, and getting other people to do the work. It's ruled by Jupiter, the planet of growth and excess and lazy self-confidence; in the West, Jupiter is named for a king among gods. Wood people go for it all, regardless of whether they can finish what they started, and everyone ends up bailing them out because they are so irresistible.

Earth

Earth energy moves slowly and is functional, practical, and reliable, organizing people to devise prudent pension arrangements as soon as they get on to solid food. It is ruled by Saturn, the planet of limitation, working hard for it all and keeping it hidden away from everyone else. Earth people lack imagination or a sense of adventure, but are very attractive to grasshoppers.

Water

Water energy flows insidiously, infiltrates and wears away rocks into the shape it desires, without the rocks noticing. It is ruled by Mercury, the planet of fast-talking, guileful thievery, taking it all and running away with it. Water people charm and fascinate, pick up telling details; they work on the emotional level, and persuade people to want to do what they want them to do.

Fire

Fire energy is aggressive, adventurous, selfish, and domineering, always pushing for action, however inappropriate. It is ruled by Mars, the planet of psychotic aggression—risking it all, losing it all, and getting it back at knife point. Fire people can be irresistibly warm and brilliant, but they can also scorch the Earth for miles around if they misdirect their energetic flame.

THE RAT

1900, 1912, 1924, 1936, 1948, 1960,
1972, 1984, 1996

FUTURE RAT: **2008**

Fixed element: **Water**

Energy: **Yang**

Hour of the Rat: **11:00 p.m.–12:59 a.m.**

Month: **December**

Season: **Winter**

Direction: **North**

Chinese name: *Shu*

The Way of the Dirty Rat

Devious, manipulative, calculating, greedy, exploitative,
restless, secretive, treacherous

IN YOUR ELEMENT

Although your fixed element is water (*see page 15*), all five Rats in the 60-year cycle spring the cheese from their traps in different ways, because each year is ruled by a different element.

WOOD RAT 1924, 1984

Lab Rat: the insinuating rodent that learns how to work the system so well that lazy technicians give you the key to the maze, and let you get on with the experiment yourself.

EARTH RAT 1948, 2008

Hardbitten rindhoarder; what's yours is yours, what's anybody else's is yours. Intolerant and self-righteous, you're obsessed with keeping up with the Joneses and upgrading to an executive sewer.

TEMPERAMENT

Eastern astrologers make a point of trying to reassure us, saying that in the East the Rat is regarded as handsome, lucky, a natural survivor, a boon to personkind, an ideal animal role model, and anybody born in the Year of the Rat has a once-in-a-lifetime chance to double their money, happiness, number of partners, and so on. This is probably because they have been got at by Rats. Remember why the Rat was first out of the cage? Because he sat on the head of the dumb Ox. And was rewarded for it: start as you mean to go on. Having learned you can get away with anything if you do it with enough chutzpah, the Rat has flourished ever since.

You Dirty Rat

What springs to the minds of the rest of us when we think of rats? Sinking ships … collaborators … opportunists … Judases … plague carriers. Always there when the grain silos are bursting, but never seen plowing the field. Give me one good reason why we should change our minds? Well, you can probably give me thousands, knowing that I would be suckered by at least one of them; because you are a cynical charmer, a con artist, and a professional wheedler. All those years your ancestors spent outwitting behavioral psychologists in the lab have paid off and now you can manipulate any data, and operate tiny levers that others don't even know are there.

THE RAT

WATER RAT 1912, 1972

Ingratiating brown-nose, sucking up to the rich and powerful and patronizing the poor. Smart manipulator, though; why row your own boat when you can make Mole beg for the privilege?

FIRE RAT 1936, 1996

King Rat: aggressive, competitive, and impatient, always ready to gnaw through the fabric of society (or the electricity cables—in which case you go out in a blaze of glory, just as you planned.)

METAL RAT 1900, 1960

The original Stainless Steel Rat, the indestructible destroyer lurking behind the Establishment baseboard, sharpening your titanium teeth ready for regime change; the Stalin of the Rat run.

The founder of the Self-Preservation Society, you did not get where you are today by not sweating the small stuff; if you ferret out the damning details, the big picture will take care of itself, you have always found. Behind that charming whisker-waggling exterior is a single-minded, omni-purpose aggressor; those sharp, pointy little teeth can scuttle any lifeboats on the sinking ship you are abandoning, or gnaw away at the self-esteem of your cagemates, destroying—invisibly but effectively—from within. You are always up for a cheap deal and would never just buy anything if there was a glimmer of a chance you could get it off the back of a truck. That's the one way the rest of us can get you: although you're a career grifter, you are a sucker for a free lunch, and the bigger the chunk of Cheddar, the blinder you are to the trap.

NOTORIOUS RATS

You may be too smart for most of us, but even you need a role model to show you how to wriggle out of sticky corners. There's a scarily large number of politicians, actors, and charlatans to choose from, but try these for inspiration.

Heinrich Himmler (b. October 7, 1900)
The Metal Rat with enough chutzpah to rat on Adolf Hitler. Toward the end of World War II, when the *Übermensch* was not quite so *über* any more, Himmler tried to broker a ceasefire on the Western Front. When Hitler found out, he expelled Himmler from the Nazi Party (see how Rats get off lightly?). After Germany surrendered, Himmler fled, but was caught; he escaped trial by committing suicide, using his secret stash of cyanide pills. A bit extreme, but impressive Ratting nevertheless.

Richard Nixon (b. January 9, 1913)
Yes, Tricky Dicky himself, wouldn't you know it—the master of the smart sidestep. A Water Rat (he should have paid more attention to hotel names). And he was a lawyer! Wheeled and dealed illegally behind the scenes, got found out, but miraculously stayed out of jail while his co-plotters didn't. Almost impeached, but scampered out of it all by resigning.

Rat Mantra
What's in it for me?

COMPANION ANIMALS

You also have an animal that sniffs around the hour of your birth (see pages 12–13 for details). According to Chinese tradition, the animal in charge of your birth hour gives you your social mask, the yang self that you present to the world.

The Hour of the Rat

11:00 p.m.–12:59 a.m.
You can afford to hurl your mask of devious charm into the garbage can with no loss of face; you're just the same old devious, charming Rat underneath.

The Hour of the Snake

9:00–10:59 a.m.
Sly, sexy, enigmatic Rat, you can slide a long, sinuous tail around the hearts and wallets of your many admirers and squeeze until they squeal.

The Hour of the Ox

1:00–2:59 a.m.
You appear solid, reliable, and even a little dull. That's exactly the look you were after for cleaning up at the all-night poker school.

The Hour of the Dragon

7:00–8:59 a.m.
Iron-willed Rat, big on generous financial gestures; luckily, your inner Rat goes around later to renegotiate.

5:00–6:59 a.m.
Neat, adorable Rat with a soft squeak; you can calculate to a whisker-width how much fluffiness and big-eye work it takes to get a meal ticket for life.

The Hour of the Tiger

3:00–4:59 a.m.
Overambitious, overconfident, loud, noisy Rat; a chance for the rest of us to part a Rat from their cash for a change.

The Hour of the Rabbit

Your native hour, the Hour of the Rat, spans midnight—late enough for you to get away with stuff under cover of night, yet early enough for rich pickings as bars and restaurants throw out their garbage.

THE RAT

The Hour of the Horse

The Hour of the Pig

The Hour of the Sheep

11:00 a.m.–12:59 p.m.
Reckless, feckless, riskophile Rat; even other Rats steer clear of you. (Rats and Horses pull in different ways, so this combination can be exploited by the rest of us.).

9:00–10:59 p.m.
Can never quite bring yourself to administer the killing nip, so always the last Rat in line for the grain bins; your kind deeds are seen as a Rat trap.

1:00–2:59 p.m.
Sentimental, sensitive, self-pitying Rat, full of sob stories designed to make the rest of us pay up, unless we get to look in your cold, beady little eyes.

7:00–8:59 p.m.
You doggedly track down the owners of any stray wallets or diamond chokers you find; expect only a modest reward.

5:00–6:59 p.m.
Stylish, strutting, elegant Rat; Rats and Roosters don't mix, so this combination can self-destruct, especially when you squander your inner Rat's secret stash on bling.

3:00–4:59 p.m.
Unbeatably smooth criminal; Rat sniffs out the opportunities, Monkey picks the locks and cracks the safe combination.

The Hour of the Dog

The Hour of the Monkey

The Hour of the Rooster

RAT
IN LOVE

The rest of the zoo falls fawning, with tedious regularity, under the onslaught of your turbocharm (except for the Horse, which makes you really mad). You've got personal magnetism by the truckload and extreme flirting is your default mode (in the Western zodiac, you twinkle along the spangled tightrope that links Gemini with Sagittarius, and boy does it show!). Addicted to romantic gestures, you are heartbreakingly sentimental, in the way gangland overlords are sentimental about their moms. As you cannot bear to be alone, squeaking into the empty night, you fall in love easily, often, and usually when still in love with someone else. You promise partners the moon on a stick, so that you can snatch it back easily when you change your mind.

Rats in Bed

Although sensual and self-indulgent, you cannot be bothered with anything involving velvet whips or warm honey; get in, get laid, get out is your motto; you like straightforward hot, sweaty sex, and you like it fast and often. Although it's all over very quickly, you are up and rutting again almost immediately. Friction burns are a real danger. (Your actual rat can reproduce once a month; be careful.)

Hot Rats

Who is the Great Rat Lover? How about Clark Gable as Rhett Butler— Scarlett O'Hara's downfall. (*Gone with the Wind* was published in 1936, so technically in the Year of the Fire Rat.) Gable was a Metal Rat (b. February 1, 1901) and Rhett was the smooth-talking rogue who, in the end, my dear, frankly didn't give a damn. And didn't we all love him for it?

And there's more ... All the rest of us will have had at least one love Rat or *Rat fatale* who has charmed their way into our hearts and then upped and left, just when we thought it was all going so well. So we know how it hurts, yet we still let internationally famous feckless charmers (Hugh Grant, Ben Affleck, Prince Charles) get away with it.

RAT DATE

Listen up, other animals. The Rat date means you pay! Lady Rats would not dream of paying, and hot restaurants are loud with Boy Rats announcing in a deprecating manner that they have left their wallet in the other Armani. Of course you pay up, unless you are a Horse. You will never get the money back, but in return the Rat will show you his/her idea of a good time. Great bars, casinos, intimate little bars, exclusive restaurants (Rats can always get into a kitchen), waterfront dives, other people's yachts, back to the first great bar, etc. Then, at the end of the evening (which may be three days later) and your credit limit, the Rat will make a few calls on your cellphone and disappear into the dawn, looking for new pickings.

MATING MISTAKES

Rat and Rat

Whiskers knot in a terrible embrace as you try to outwit each other, and the experiment has to be abandoned.

Rat and Ox

Don't be fooled by the solid plodding; when they catch you playing away, they'll crush you under their great hooves.

Rat and Tiger

Your charm is not strong enough to hold them down, plus they get irritated by your gnawing little ways. The tiger is just a big cat; and you know what cats think of you.

Rat and Rabbit *

If in Rabbit mode, a clash of rodent gnashers is unavoidable; if in Cat mode, never forget a cat is just a Tiger seen from far away.

Rat and Dragon

Of course, they are way out of your league, but you don't think they are, and almost have them fooled for a moment.

Rat and Snake

You do charm and fascination, but they do fatal charm and fascination; guess who ends up marinating in whose gastric juices?

Rat and Horse

Don't even think about trying to insinuate yourself into this nosebag; they'll drop-kick you right out of the stable.

Rat and Sheep *

If they are in Sheep mode, their pitiful baaing bores you rigid; if they are Goatish, you'll be headbutted out of the way to make room for someone who delivers the luxury goods.

Rat and Monkey

Smarter, cleverer, and quicker than you, with more dextrous digits and opposable thumbs.

Rat and Rooster

You stare at them with your beady little eyes; they stare at you with their beady little eyes; you won't win this one, because they can henpeck you into submission.

Rat and Dog

Is this really a good idea? Although all dogs are not terriers, all terriers are dogs; find a drainpipe a.s.a.p.

Rat and Pig

Your natural prey; Pigs fall for your charm every time, which is no fun because you need stimulation and challenge.

* For inscrutable Eastern reasons, the Rabbit is also known as the Cat, and the Sheep as the Goat.

THE RAT

RAT AT WORK

As a rootless opportunist, you thrive in the market economy, working freelance (it doesn't matter much what as) launching fail-safe scams and schemes to satisfy your endless lust for money. When they fail—as they will because you suffer from Chronic Overstretch Syndrome and stick your little paws into way too many pies—you always get out the back door just as the repo men come in the front, and pop up under another name in another state with another plausible plan. However, if you work for yourself, you can't very well shaft the boss, so many of you take your raging ambition for a scamper up the corporate ladder, greasing the rungs as you go, to foil any backstabber (usually another Rat) who is following. On the way, you sweet-talk killer ideas out of unwary colleagues and present them as your own. Vengeful victims may set a honey trap for you, and as the sweet scent of a fast buck always overrides your seventh sense (danger), you often fall in; but every self-respecting Rat has an exit strategy, so you don't stay there for long. (Note for the rest of us: keep an eye on Rat colleagues, for they always sense when the Board is about to skip town with the pension fund.)

Office Politics

There probably wouldn't be any office politics if you weren't out there fomenting unrest, spreading gossip, schmoozing, and backstabbing. You take uglier, dumber colleagues out to lunch, ferret out their secrets and information they didn't know they had, then use it against them.

TIME BANDIT	OFFICE INFECTOR	ASSET STRIPPER
Rarely seen at your workstation, you know to the second when to pop out from behind the baseboard for that important meeting, or when the CEO is meeting and greeting.	Your duvet days reach double figures, but as you always get the work done (you charm Pigs into doing it for you), management is reluctant to incur the lawsuit that will follow if they fire you.	Everyone jacks a bit of office stationery; you persuade the supplier to deliver wholesale to your home, then sell it to college kids at a keen price—any mark-up on zero must be good.

Rat Boss

You are great at bossing, because you know all about carrots and sticks, and if you're a really smart rodent, you don't even need the carrot, because you can charm work out of your drudges, then throw a magnificent hissy fit when they ask for a living wage, and sack them all. No loss; as CEO of Rats 'r' Us (a company owned by one of your dead grandmothers), you file for Chapter II on Thursday; on Friday you launch Ratbucks, Inc.

Rat Slacker

No one doubts your industry, but management is deluded if they think you'd waste all that energy on their behalf. You work very hard at everything but the actual job in hand, because you are usually running your own thriving import-export business on the side, courtesy of your company's software, delivery systems, etc.

Rat 9–5er

Not the first choice for stickability, loyalty, and mindless following of orders. Show you a system and you can't wait to subvert it. You're way too twitchy to plod, and you never clock-watch, mainly because you haven't yet lurched back from your good old fashioned three-Martini lunch.

Suitable Jobs for Rats

Lawyer

Actor

Pimp

Politician

Spin doctor

Used-car dealer

Gossip columnist

RAT AT HOME

Rat Habitat

This is usually a temporary structure—it may be just your car, or a set of Italian leather luggage. You hate to be tied down, or pay rent, so the nest of choice will be a squat, a houseshare, an unlicenced RV, or your new best friend's fashionable grain loft. If you do find a more permanent space, it soon clutters up with stuff you snapped up at the thrift store, reclaimed from the dump, borrowed from friends, or could not resist because it was a bargain—you are obsessive-accumulative.

Rat Neighbors

Despite being a passing ship in the night, you are the nosiest of neighbors, twitching the drapes and tracking any action with the night-vision binos you picked up at the Langley yard sale, bringing a whole new meaning to the term neighborhood security. The local PD would love your database if they did not already suspect you of most local crime. You monger the kind of rumors that would turn Sesame Street into a war zone, but move on before it all gets critical.

Feeding Habits

You're an omnivore, so you eat and drink anything—especially if it's free or someone else has paid for it. When you eat out, you order the cheapest thing on the menu (or nothing at all), then take increasingly large nibbles of everybody else's food. Your specialty is the last french fry, eaten directly from your neighbor's plate. You never want pizza when your housemates place the order, but always get the biggest slice when it arrives.

Rat Roomie

People who share with you must have a Zen approach to the possession of possessions. You turn up as Prince(ss) Charming, but once in, you will borrow your roomie's Jimmy Choos and leave one of them in the park, slap on their Coco de Mer moisturizer and leave the lid off, overload the washing machine, and ignore the chore list. When challenged, you mock them for being so anal; if they use any of your stuff, you bite them. They will need a subpoena to get your share of the rent out of you.

Rat Runs

The essential Rat hideout must have an easy getaway route and an uninterrupted supply of food and drink; so, anywhere with a back door or three, storage for all your borrowed stuff, and paid for by someone else.

* Houseboat
* Converted loft
* Motel
* RV
* Airport terminal
* Luxury penthouse apartment with your own elevator

THE OX

(Also called the Buffalo, but that doesn't make you any more exciting)

1901, 1913, 1925, 1937, 1949, 1961,

1973, 1985, 1997

FUTURE OX: **2009**

Fixed element: **Water**	
Energy: **Yin**	
Hour of the Ox: **1:00–2:59 a.m.**	
Month: **January**	
Season: **Winter**	
Direction: **North-northeast**	
Chinese name: *Niu*	

The Way of the Plodding Ox

Intractable, inflexible, stubborn, relentless, opinionated, dull, dogmatic, extremist, judgmental, narrow-minded

Although your fixed element is Water (*see page 15*), all five Oxen in the 60-year cycle plow a slightly different furrow, because each year is ruled by a different element.

Skittish Ox, who has heard of the word "change" and understands that there are other people, and that to succeed you have to be seen to be taking their pitiful ideas into consideration.

No retreat, baby, no surrender. Always the Last Man Standing, mainly because you have your four feet firmly stuck into mud that was fresh when dinosaurs roamed the Earth.

TEMPERAMENT

There's not much I can say here, for even Eastern astrologers have you down as resolute and stubborn, although they dress it up with words like cautious and dependable, protest that you are not at all slow-witted, and claim you always give good, solid advice—but fail to say this is about the wisdom of buying an all-inclusive pension-insurance-death-benefit scheme from your company. The Ox comes second in the animal zodiac. It would have come first (you are big, strong, ambitious, and unstoppable when traveling in a straight line), but was comprehensively outclassed by the wily Rat, because the Ox does not do wit, guile, or rapid response.

Bully for You

Some authorities classify you as a Buffalo, but that doesn't really lighten the load, because it still means that you won't move unless prodded with a sharp, pointed stick, and won't jump quickly enough to get out of the way of the white man's rifle; you think standing up to your knees in mud staring at nothing in particular is a great night out.

Extreme conviction and commitment are what you like. It doesn't much matter what you are committed to: you can change your mind completely (but very, very slowly) and commit resolutely to another extreme. Because you don't care what others think, you are unscathed when people say you are a traitor to the cause. They are wrong.

WATER OX 1913, 1973

Slightly diluted Ox, dimly aware of other furrows. However, yours is still The Way, so you wear down any opposition with slow, patient drips, just like water torture.

FIRE OX 1937, 1997

Vesuvius in slo-mo, tact-free and ready to blow without warning. Even more mighty and righty than the rest of the herd, and voted the Ox most likely to be killed by his or her own troops.

METAL OX 1901. 1961

Fundamentalist fanatic, tough of hide and mind. Welded to your guns, you bellow down any opposition and take no prisoners. Failure is not an option, and vengeance is always yours.

You are always right. Others make mistakes; you never do. You know only one direction—and that is forward until you hit the wall, when you tramp agreeably on the spot until a kindly Rooster turns you to face in another direction and you plod forth. It is impossible for you to back down about anything (have you ever seen a plow go backward?).

They say you are born to be led, but that's not strictly true, is it? Of course you can wear the yoke, but you'd much rather be bellowing orders and brandishing the whip; but you can wait. You start believing in your ineluctable destiny (don't you, Hitler, Napoleon, Saddam?). Your great shoulders are wide enough to bear an infinite number of grudges, but then you do plow the lonely leyline that links Capricorn and Cancer in the Western zodiac, which also explains your insatiable love of food and money.

NOTORIOUS OXEN

Even though you are always right, and no one tells you what to do without being trampled, you may appreciate a few pointers from the Ox masters. Out of a large field of world dictators, emperors, and method actors, consider the following.

Adolf Hitler (b. April 20, 1889)

Low on talent, but off the scale on will and determination, Hitler barged stolidly through obstacles that would have stopped more thoughtful animals, and almost got to his goal of a thousand-year empire and a much larger paddock. Obstinately obsessed by the glory of a tall, blond, blue-eyed world of heroes, even though he was a short, dark, blue-eyed dictator, he lost out because he would not compromise, surrender, or listen to advice from people who knew.

Margaret Thatcher (b. October 13, 1925)

Another world-class example of high-end recalcitrance yoked with unshakable self-belief. The Iron Lady was Prime Minister of the UK (1979–90) and throughout her seemingly endless term insisted: a) there was no alternative; b) she was not for turning; and c) there was no such thing as society. Many people agreed with her, as it was easier—and strangely comforting.

Ox Mantra

We'll do it my way

COMPANION ANIMALS

You also have an animal that sniffs around the hour of your birth (see pages 12–13 for details). According to Chinese tradition, the animal in charge of your birth hour gives you your social mask, the yang self that you present to the world.

The Hour of the Rat

The Hour of the Snake

The Hour of the Ox

The Hour of the Dragon

The Hour of the Tiger

The Hour of the Rabbit

11:00 p.m.–12:59 a.m.
Party bovine; some grains of small talk here, a nifty hoof, and a passing interest in other people. Other Oxen consider you rather flashy and inconsequential.

1:00–2:59 a.m.
Not the Ox to meet on a dark night. Remember *Full Metal Jacket*? Gunnery Sergeant Hartman? You make him look like a bereavement counselor.

3:00–4:59 a.m.
Ferocious Ox, swathing through society like a war chariot with blade-runner wheels; the Ox always wins in the end.

5:00–6:59 a.m.
Refined Ox, with a gingham-lined manger and a whim of iron. Often so busy piecing your Martha Stewart-style quilted yoke throw that you don't have time for the plow.

7:00–8:59 a.m.
Flamboyant, conceited Ox, so far ahead of the herd that you are first to thunder over the precipice and crash below.

9:00–10:59 a.m.
Enigmatic Ox; you actually appear as mysterious as your inner Ox thinks you are. Last seen swishing down a dark sidestreet in a long black leather coat.

Your native hour, the Hour of the Ox, runs from one o'clock to three in the morning—the small hours when nothing much seems to be going on, there are few loud noises or uncomfortable changes, and plenty of time for cud chewing.

牛 THE OX

The Hour of the Horse

11:00 a.m.–12:59 p.m.
Your hooves won't stop twinkling, your yoke makes you itchy, you just know you could jump the picket fence if you wanted, and your furrows are all zigzags. And you don't care.

The Hour of the Pig

9:00–10:59 p.m.
Slacker Ox, you are easily bribed to take on extra work because you don't like saying no to anything that involves extra rations.

The Hour of the Sheep

1:00–2:59 p.m.
Sheep and Oxen don't mix; your inner Dutiful Plodder gets hacked off having to carry your outer Woolly Minded Hedonist home from a night on the *caparinhas*.

The Hour of the Dog

7:00–8:59 p.m.
Fundamentalist do-gooder with your own spike-lined yoke; you wonder how much you could charge for all that fundraising.

5:00–6:59 p.m.
Mouthy Ox, you strut around declaiming how you are going to fight City Hall, the management, etc. (it doesn't matter why); actually go and fight, win a long war of attrition, then crow about it.

The Hour of the Monkey

3:00–4:59 p.m.
Smart, slick Ox, with neat little hooves that can switch the dice, palm the cards, and fix the roulette wheel.

The Hour of the Rooster

OX
IN LOVE

Love, Lord above, don't let's go there. You are scared of love. Quite right, too: it's unsettling and disrupts routine. If love does strike, it just makes you stand even stiller in your paddock until it goes away. Admirers should prepare to be underwhelmed. For a start, they will have to make the first move and should expect to be ignored (unless they are obscenely rich). You may very well be smitten to your beefy core, but you would never, ever tell the object of your affection, or turn up with a surprise present (or even turn up). Deluded lovers read this as playing hard-to-get, so some Oxen get an undeserved rep for mystery. Away from the jungle of amour, however, you are very sound on marriage, a wonderful institution guaranteed to put an end to any love nonsense, once and for all.

Ox in Bed

You don't really understand the seduction game, because it's full of nuance, with nothing to put your hoof on. Sex, though, is a different matter. You are solid and powerful and sexy, in a way large trucks and big rigs are. Also, sex is controllable, pleasurable exercise and imperative for your dynastic plans. Any spontaneous passion can easily be melted away by rigorous timetabling.

Hot Oxen

Let's hear it for Napoleon Bonaparte (b. 1769)—not an obvious choice, but think about it: he relentlessly pursued serial-mistress-to-leading-politicos Josephine de Beauharnais, partly because he loved her and partly because she was a great career asset. He was younger, shorter, and lower-born, but did not stop until she married him. Instructed her on just how he liked his sex life; left her only because she could not produce the heir to satisfy his imperial longings. Serious Oxing, I think you'll agree.

And there's more … A surprising number of Oxen are very cute, and probably prefer to think of themselves as Buffaloes (Gary Cooper, Paul Newman, Robert Redford). Aging, self-styled Hollywood Bad Boys Jack Nicholson and Warren Beatty are both 1937 Fire Oxen.

牛 THE OX

OX DATE

If you get a date with an Ox (and be honest—it's the bulging wallet or sheer physicality that attracted you), it will be because you have made it. Oxen never make the first move, because it involves talking to others and trying to empathize. There won't be any flowers or candy, unless you bring them yourself (and then the Ox will eat the candy). The Ox will not ask you where you would like to go, but will have booked a table at a favorite steakhouse. The evening will be endless, as the Ox lectures you on the intricacies of tort law, sound investment strategy, or their timetable for world domination. You may be surprised to discover that it is still light outside. If the Ox has to fulfill his or her exercise quota, you may have vigorous sex. They will never call afterward, because they expect you to be available, same time, same place, next week—and all the weeks into the future. If you don't show, they know where you live. You may need an injunction.

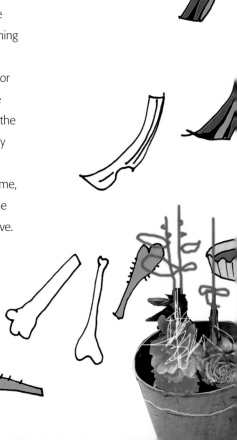

MATING MISTAKES

THE OX

Ox and Rat
They will bedazzle you and encourage you to try some of your ponderous flirting; then bring their friends around and make fun of you.

Ox and Ox
Yoked together side by side, you can't actually see each other, so you carry on behaving as if you are alone. Neither of you notices.

Ox and Tiger
It's all a blur of stripes and teeth—and then they're gone. You could pretend the scratch marks were dueling scars, if you had any imagination, that is.

Ox and Rabbit
How gratifying! They agree with your every plan, especially the one where you set up charge accounts for them, so that they can buy you presents.

Ox and Dragon
Your dull treasures don't impress them, and they will barbecue your heart with just one kiss, and eat it, possibly on a bed of fava beans.

Ox and Snake
You are naive; you let them curl up in the company's cash vault. You can't even begin to explain it to the police.

Ox and Horse
You like bracing exercise as much as the next hoofed mammal, but they will be up, off, and running before you can get back into your pjs.

Ox and Sheep
There is no way you are sharing your lush field with someone who can nibble paradise into a desert, without even thinking about it.

Ox and Monkey
For the first time in your life you get a faint idea of what fun might be about. Then Monkey runs away with the circus.

Ox and Rooster
You might love the feel of them strutting up and down your broad back, massaging your spine, but they will peck your eyes out, if you don't come up with the treatment fee.

Ox and Dog
They drive you into a corner and bark themselves hoarse about animal rights all night. No skin off your nose—you're not listening.

Ox and Pig
A mutual delight in large meals isn't enough, especially as you suspect they have a bigger feeding trough than you do.

OX AT WORK

If it wasn't for you, planet Work would stop spinning. You are right, but you have zero people skills and fail to realize, or care, that the rest of us don't want to be reminded about it quite so often. You are the work engine of the rural economy that sustains most of the world, which gives you an enormous sense of smug self-worth. You may keep your eyes down when working, but that doesn't mean you are modest and easily dominated. Work is what you do; and whatever you do is work—even if it is play (as those of us who played Monopoly with you and now live in a cardboard box know the cost). You don't do innovation, brainstorming, or lateral thinking, although if someone leads you to an exciting new furrow, straps your harness on, and slaps you on the butt, you can go off fairly happily in another direction. If you own the company, your only real game plan is to carry on.

You've got to accumulate to accumulate, you believe, so you will never let anything go, the company gets big and unwieldy, and smart Rats slide in to strip it to the bone.

Office Politics

Hopeless. You have no grasp of guile, tact, or diplomacy, or any kind of strategy that involves sidesteps. In a confrontation you just make your point and stand there blocking the path until distracted. The devious think your strong-and-silent act is a cunning ruse, but you are strong and silent because you only have six ideas in your head that revolve slowly like shark's teeth.

TIME BANDIT	OFFICE INFECTOR	ASSET STRIPPER
You don't know how, and you would not want to, as it would disrupt your routine. You're the one found bolt upright and dead as a doornail at your workstation.	Infector general. You disdain weakness and never get sick. Even if you do, it would take another two teams of oxen to prevent you plowing on.	You know exactly how many pushpins are in the stock room, and would not borrow a single one. But you go for lock, stock, and barrel for whole countries.

Ox Boss

Yes, yes, yes. Discipline. Authority. Your word is law. You love issuing directives and then coming round to check they have been followed to the letter. You are red-hot on detail, and there is no board meeting you won't hold up by plowing through the minutiae of canteen entitlements organized by rank, or who has rights to which washroom. If it all goes wrong, you don't hesitate to blame your workforce and vote yourself a substantial salary hike.

Ox Slacker

You have no grasp of the grasshopper mentality. It may look as though you're slacking, but that is only because you take a very long time to complete any task to your satisfaction and loathe shortcuts. Deadline-chasing colleagues want to kill you.

Ox 9–5er

Only slightly less exciting than being boss, because following orders is your next-favorite hobby. However, you like your routine, and if 9–5 is what it says on the tin, that's what you do. If the place is burning down at clocking-off time, you clock off. It is not in your job description to freelance as a firefighter.

Suitable Jobs for Oxen

World dictator   Despot   Police chief   Loss adjuster

Ordinary dictator   Dominatrix
                     Henchperson   General

OX AT HOME

Ox Habitat

Home is where it has always been, because you hate to move far from the farm. You like plenty of space between you and prying neighbors, so a log cabin in the middle of the prairie or a 'burb with a blinding-white picket fence showing exactly where your domain ends and the world begins. You'd really like to go back to the Old Ways and live above the shop (even if you are a merchant banker) so that you can keep an eye on all your possessions.

Ox Neighbors

Other people are noisy and bothersome, so you ignore them; and as you don't do small talk, you have no idea who your neighbors are, and get grouchy when the cops come around asking if you heard gunshots in the night. However, should anyone come up your fiercely trimmed path without an appointment, looking for a shoulder to cry on or a cup of sugar, you will chase them off with your Winchester pump, because you are one with Charlton Heston on this.

Feeding Habits

You have a favorite food and you eat it, regularly. If your usual diner does not have your usual meal on the menu, or it tastes any different, you storm out, headbutting the chef on the way. This is why you prefer chain restaurants. You prefer to dine alone, because you have noticed that having other people around, talking and laughing, wastes good eating and drinking time. At a dinner party you are the one face down in the trough while the table coruscates with Wildean wit.

Ox Roomie

This only works if the other roomies are spineless, on permanent vacation, or loved up on E. Dragons may put up initial opposition, but you will win in the end because you stand still until you get your way. (This may not work if your other roomies are Oxen.) Whatever the house rules, you follow your house rules. You do your share of the chores, but follow everyone around when it's their shift, to make sure they do things just like you do. You don't worry about rent; you usually own the place.

Ox Stalls

The essential Ox pasture should be substantial, extensive, and have highly visible borders and a top security system. There should be only one, defensible door.

* Brownstone block (all of it)
* Ranch
* Fort Knox
* Williamsburg, Virginia
* Prison yard

THE TIGER

1902, 1914, 1926, 1938, 1950, 1962,
1974, 1986, 1998

FUTURE TIGER: **2010**

Fixed Element: **Wood**

Energy: **Yang**

Hour of the Tiger: **3:00–4:59 a.m.**

Month: **February**

Season: **Winter**

Direction: **East-northeast**

Chinese name: *Hu*

The Way of the Snarling Tiger

Rebellious, unpredictable, impatient, violent,
extreme, headstrong, obstinate, restless, reckless,
suspicious, attention-seeking, egocentric

WOOD TIGER 1914, 1974

EARTH TIGER 1938, 1998

Although your fixed element is Wood (*see page 15*), all five Tigers in the 60-year cycle bounce to individual rhythms, because each year is ruled by a different element.

Captive Tiger, willing to appear tame and docile, if that's what it takes to get you out of the cage. You purr politely, ask everyone for their opinion, then do what you were going to do anyway.

Siberian Tiger, you burn at a slightly lower wattage because you are saving energy, which means you can focus long enough to work out which of your admirers will be most useful.

TEMPERAMENT

Asian astrologers really rate the cosmic White Tiger, considered the embodiment of luck and dynamism, the bringer of bouncy good fortune, and destroyer of the darkside. All those who can ride the tiger, or even just Velcro themselves to its tail, will flourish and, even if they don't—well, it's an honor and a privilege to be eaten alive by such a splendid beast. The Tiger was the third animal to cross the river to Buddha—probably because he was too busy showing off complicated swimming strokes that took up all his energy, or wouldn't listen to advice about local conditions and wasted time swimming against the current.

Tiger, Tiger!

Having someone born in the Year of the Tiger in the home apparently works like a high-end comprehensive insurance policy that protects against fire, theft, and evil spirits. This kind of executive multitasking—ghostbuster, firefighter, and vigilante all in one—is exactly what Tigers like best. Yes, but what about the claw marks on the furniture and the door hanging off its hinges where you burst in to save the day?

While most people like the idea of tigers, it's just a little bit sweaty having you restlessly pacing up and down, wired with self-generated adrenalin and getting in the way while they try to defrost the freezer. Just think how tedious Tigger is. Fortunately, you

虎 THE TIGER

WATER TIGER 1902, 1962

Stuffed Tiger. You may have your claws trimmed, your teeth filed down, and a regular scrip for Ritalin, but those who think you're just a big pussycat should recall that Tigers never lose their stripes.

FIRE TIGER 1926, 1986

Circus Tiger. There is only one show in town, and you're the self-obsessed star, flickering in and out of people's lives on your way to the moon, the Mariana Trench, or the top of Mt McKinley.

METAL TIGER 1950. 2010

Sabre-toothed Tiger, born to be wild. You want it all, you want it now—and who would be numbnut enough to face up to those shiny fangs and stop you, even if it is for your own good.

have the attention span of a mayfly and the tenacity of wet lettuce, so don't stay too long in one spot. Fueled by inexhaustible self-belief and a Texas-sized ego, there is no missing you—and that is the plan. All that single-handed snatching of curly-haired tinies from the jaws of death is just for your fix of fame and glory (fortune is an optional plus). You insist on living life to the full, even if it kills you—and several innocent bystanders.

Tigers live two lives at once, trying to reconcile an existential contradiction: headstrong and indecisive at the same time, you are a kind of executive procrastinator, a fizzing energy source not quite hooked up to the switch. In the Western zodiac, you prowl along the jungle path that links Leo, the attention junkie, with Aquarius, the eccentric loner. This means that while you have to be a leader, you don't really care if no one follows.

NOTORIOUS TIGERS

Naturally, every Tiger is a celebrity, because Tigerdom is all about self, but some Tigers burn more brightly than others. Out of a stellar cast of monarchs, captains of industry, rebels, daredevils, film stars, and hard-drinking boho poets, give it up for:

虎 THE TIGER

Robert Craig "Evel" Knievel
(b. October 17, 1938)

Relentless stuntman, who made a very successful career out of pointlessly jumping over long rows of parked cars and buses on his motorcycle, often through flaming hoops. Constantly injured, he turned his singular skill into a moneyspinning market success. But, even better, his achievements made him a regular in the *Guinness Book of World Records*. Everlasting fame! Tiger nirvana.

Karl Marx (b. May 5, 1818)

Professional revolutionary, Marx dashed off the *Communist Manifesto* (1848) in six weeks in superb Tiger mode. An executive philosopher ("philosophers have only interpreted the world in various ways; the point is, to change it"), Marx gypsied all over Europe and ended his days caged in the British Museum, failing to finish his great work, *Das Kapital*.

Tiger Mantra
Look at me!

COMPANION ANIMALS

You also have an animal that sniffs around the hour of your birth (see pages 12–13 for details). According to Chinese tradition, the animal in charge of your birth hour gives you your social mask, the yang self that you present to the world.

The Hour of the Rat

11:00 p.m.–12:59 a.m.
Why bother to storm the barricades, teeth gleaming, when you can flirt or bribe your way around and get the same result, without the heroic dying bit.

The Hour of the Snake

9:00–10:59 a.m.
Cool, smooth, and suspicious on the outside; loud, growly, and suspicious on the inside. Good cop, bad cop—all in one package.

The Hour of the Ox

1:00–2:59 a.m.
Fearful symmetry does not even come close. Ox and Tiger don't blend, but your outer Ox will force you to get your stripes in a row.

The Hour of the Dragon

7:00–8:59 a.m.
Exhausting high achiever, forever driving your people onward; they are secretly advertising for a dragon slayer.

5:00–6:59 a.m.
Serene, plush tiger, content to sit in the sun all day; everyone is really surprised when you turn on your trainer with a killer bite to the neck.

The Hour of the Tiger

3:00–4:59 a.m.
Nothing short of the heat-death of the cosmos will stop you going supernova; but at least you'll die pretty.

The Hour of the Rabbit

Your native hour, the Hour of the Tiger, runs from three o'clock to five in the morning, the darkest hours before dawn, just the time to lead your platoon on a foolhardy raid of the enemy's ammo dump.

虎 THE TIGER

* For inscrutable Eastern reasons, the Sheep is also known as the Ram or Goat.

The Hour of the Horse

The Hour of the Pig

The Hour of the Sheep

11:00 a.m.–12:59 p.m.
Practical and handy, yet irresponsible and reckless, which means that at least your backyard rocket launcher and indoor jet skis are perfectly maintained and ready to go.

9:00–10:59 p.m.
Sugar tiger, too idle to do much pouncing, but in popular demand as a lovable brand figure for the more tooth-rotting breakfast cereals.

1:00–2:59 p.m.
Your outer Ram (or Goat)* makes you just one big cat on a hot tin roof; you don't mind as you love the smell of hot fur in the afternoon.

7:00–8:59 p.m.
You round up lost sheep, or growl about the farm burning down, but people panic and reach for their tranquillizer darts—or worse.

5:00–6:59 p.m.
Top in self-promotion, but you never fail to dilute the moment by stopping in mid-spring to deliver a critique of your actions and motives.

3:00–4:59 p.m.
Mastermind with muscle; how lucky it is for the rest of us that you loathe each other and won't cooperate.

The Hour of the Dog

The Hour of the Monkey

The Hour of the Rooster

TIGER IN LOVE

Tigers are always in love. If no one else is around, there is always that gorgeous beast in the mirror. But there is always someone around, because you are irresistible (self-belief makes you magnetically attractive, even if you have a face like a hamburger bun and the body of Mr. Potato Head), dashing, hot-headed, and impetuous, just as a Great Lover should be. It's all about you and the grand gesture. Your eye is caught across a crowded room; regardless of the prey's current relationship status, you pursue them relentlessly—for years if necessary, because you love stalking gazelles. Once you have your great velvety paws around their heart, the game is up. It could take a day, a week, or a year, but you will be off after the next exhilarating adventure.

Tiger in Bed

Scorched sheets of course, but it's all about Tiger gratification, so partners should not expect to be asked if they have any preferences (or even asked). You pounce when and where you feel like it: no waiting around to attune your body clocks, or even get a room. After a record-breaking 100-yard dash, Tigers—like all cats—fall asleep. However, they're ready to run again very quickly.

Hot Tiger

Romeo Montague. He may be fictional, but he's a true Tiger (as is Leo DiCaprio, who played him in Baz Luhrmann's film). An ardent street fighter, Romeo is passionately in love with the fair Rosalind when he meets Juliet, the daughter of his father's bitterest enemy. Within 10 lines of dialogue, he has kissed her and fallen passionately in love, and in the next scene he is shinning up balconies and risking life and limb to see her. Two days later he has killed himself for love—not a moment too soon, because on Tiger time he was about to lose interest.

And there's more … Where shall I start? There's no sexual dimorphism in Tigers, and Tiger women are just as magnetic and powerful as the men— is that not so, Marilyn Monroe, Demi Moore, Kate Moss?

虎 THE TIGER

TIGER DATE

Take extra vitamins. You will be besieged by ardent txtmsgs and extravagant gifts; there will be midnight yowling and threatened dramatic suicides (they will base-jump from the John Hancock Tower without a 'chute, swallow bamboo shards, set themselves alight on the steps of MOMART) until you agree to a date. (They may turn up nude with a rose between their teeth.) For a while, it will be like living in a cheesy 1950s musical, as they burst into song whenever you are together, fill your workplace with flowers and champagne, and generally tell the world that you are theirs. While in love they are fiercely jealous and passionately possessive, and will lash you to the bedposts with your own heartstrings. Sadly, they are inclined to leave you there when the flame has dimmed, which will not take long. Before the lilies have had time to droop, you can't raise them on the phone. In two weeks' time, you think you must have dreamed it all.

MATING MISTAKES

Tiger and Rat
Your inner cat can't help recalling at a cellular level that they're just a big mouse, something fussy and annoying that needs a good swat.

Tiger and Ox
You swing into their lives on your customary jungle vine, ready to bedazzle and begone, but they cut your rope, you fall into their trap, and you never get out.

Tiger and Tiger
This town ain't big enough for the both of you, even if it is greater Los Angeles. One of you lone itchy-fingered gunslingers will have to go.

Tiger and Rabbit
They make you feel like Tom Kitten trussed into a too-small suit. You make them feel they are in the wrong part of the zoo.

Tiger and Dragon
Bonnie and Clyde? Thelma and Louise? Who knows what you might get up to if you weren't fighting to the death over who wears the pants.

Tiger and Snake
You suspect they are cheating; they suspect you are; you both lie in the long grass staring at each other until one of you gives up. (It won't be them.)

Tiger and Horse
They've got slightly better reflexes, so move on even faster than you can—annoying because the rule is that you dump first.

Tiger and Sheep
You will not be able to resist gobbling this one up in one go, and then feeling ashamed of your unsportin' behavior because they were such easy meat.

Tiger and Monkey
Monkeys know how to ride you, and you love having your fur groomed. But then they tease you, and you lose your temper and roar and look foolish.

Tiger and Rooster
Two giant egos will not fit into such a small basket—plus they keep pecking away at your grand designs until they look like a fishnet.

Tiger and Dog
They just will not accept that the thrill has gone, and follow you around loyally until it seems kinder just to devour them whole.

Tiger and Pig
Your favorite, especially marinated in Napa Valley's finest and stuffed with raspberries. However, they don't digest that easily and come back to haunt you.

TIGER AT WORK

Tigers do not do work; you do missions, adventures, quests, covert ops, explorations. Actually, it doesn't matter much what, as long as you are in charge of the action—chief, captain, master and commander, trail boss, queen, star. Although you are much in demand for dawn raids and hostile takeovers, the corporate world can't handle you: you are a liability at meetings, which you consider a waste of time because, once you have made your point, you don't have the patience to listen to anyone else's; paperwork is what you use to line your litter tray; and by the time any green-light decisions have come down to you, you've abandoned the project. Most companies soon realize this and send you into the field on permanent R&D, or as troubleshooter for their less-refined operations, then get a bit edgy when you bound back in to debrief, covered in oil stains and dried blood. You would die (or kill) rather than admit to any limitations, and those who criticize your working methods will be found in ER.

Office Politics

You don't usually stay long enough in one place to get involved in petty backstabbing and jockeying for position. Anyway, you can never remember who badmouthed whom, or why, or what side you're meant to be on. Of course people are always trying to get you on their side—after all, who's going to take on 500 pounds of clawed muscle, even metaphorically?—but you never commit, because the only person who matters to you is you. It's better for everybody if you are self-employed.

TIME BANDIT	OFFICE INFECTOR	ASSET STRIPPER
Your time is your own, despite harassment by micro-minded bean counters. It's not as if you don't put in the hours … just not the same hours as everyone else.	Outstanding! Can be counted on to bounce in, back from your tropical minibreak, awash with exciting new deadly bacteria for which there is no antibody.	Negligible petty thievery, but you might inadvertently fuse all the electronic hardware in the office, and for three blocks around, by sheer personal magnetism.

Tiger Boss

Of course you're the boss, even if it isn't your actual job title. Your preferred management style is roaring and bullying, but when you are trying to inspire, you love telling rookies how you fought your way up from the tough South Side, or the cabin made of earth and wood—even if you didn't. You're rarely in the boardroom and take all your conference calls in a hot-air balloon or hanging from a crampon halfway up Annapurna. Staff dread the all-action team-bonding weekends you organize so tirelessly.

Tiger Slacker

"If only," sigh your underlings, as you bully them on to smashing the record-breaking performance targets so that you will win CEO of the Year (again) and get your picture in the company magazine.

Tiger 9–5er

This is not what Tigers do. You spend one day pacing up and down miserably in your temporal cage, escape with a roar at quitting time, and are never seen again. Forensic experts are called in to work out just how you sabotaged the filing system and what on earth your password could have been.

虎 THE TIGER

Suitable Jobs for Tigers

Supervillain

Gangster No. 1

Samurai

Getaway driver   Drug runner

Daredevil

Stuntperson

Chief (of anything)

TIGER AT HOME

Tiger Habitat

You can always spot a cage, however rose-entwined the bars, so your idea of luxury living is a backpack, a motorcycle, and the key to a lockup self-store around your neck. If you get stuck inside four walls, or the Airstream is in the shop, you redecorate obsessively in increasingly eccentric styles (Pacific Rim Gothic?) to make it feel like you're moving on. As far as you're concerned, a small, cleansing fire is the best way to declutter and improve your chi. U-Haul loves you.

Tiger Neighbors

As with everything, you start off full of enthusiasm, glowing with a hard, gemlike flame of purpose, organize the neighbors, establish a neighborhood watch team with you as its chief, set up a tenants' association with you as director, lead the rush on City Hall to get squatters' rights, then lose interest, disappear in the night, and leave everyone dazed and in some cases homeless. Unfairly, you get remembered as some kind of legendary Davy Crockett figure.

Feeding Habits

You are either gnawing raw water-buffalo steaks under a shady bush or making a stew of poke salad, owl pellets, and C-rations under enemy fire. As you have learned on your travels, everything can be eaten—and you will eat anything. One-pot cooking is ideal (the whole lot, including after-dinner mints, in one handy dish to save time). Urban Tigers are always the first into the new ethnic restaurant on the block, but usually dine alone because few people can eat as fast as you.

Tiger Roomie

Few people could resist you when you show up on the doorstep, a stray pussycat on steroids. You entertain the whole house into the small hours with your ripping yarns (some of which may even be true), and everybody gets altered states-ish on the fermented yak's milk you brought back from your last mission. You do your share of the more exciting chores, but have usually left town before rent day. Who's going to chase after you for it, except maybe an Ox?

Tiger Lairs

The essential Tiger space has to have no boundaries and endless possibilities. So a small country, a mobile home, or a paw-à-terre in every time zone.

* Winnebago
* Arizona
* Yurt
* Safari park
* Budget hotel

虎 THE TIGER

THE RABBIT

(Also known as the Hare; sometimes works under the name of Cat)

1903, 1915, 1927, 1939, 1951, 1963,
1975, 1987, 1999

FUTURE RABBIT: **2011**

Fixed element: **Wood**

Energy: **Yin**

Hour of the Rabbit: **5:00-6:59 a.m.**

Month: **March**

Season: **Spring**

Direction: **East**

Chinese name: *Tu*

The Way of the Tricksy Rabbit

Conniving, sly, conceited, plausible, hypocritical,
self-serving, smug, cold-hearted, insincere, scheming, superficial

WOOD RABBIT 1915, 1975

EARTH RABBIT 1939, 1999

Although your fixed element is Wood (*see page 15*), all five Rabbits (or Cats) in the 60-year cycle deceive the eye in different ways, because each year is ruled by a different element.

Rabbit caught in the headlights; you are too timid to decide which way to jump off the fence, so you get stuck in the middle of the road, where you are mown down by traffic.

Wild Rabbit, always in full survival mode, and fully focused on getting the greenstuff into the burrow, regardless of how many baby bunnies you have to kick out to make room.

TEMPERAMENT

Now this is a bit confusing, but then you like a bit of distraction—it takes your victim's eyes off the small print. In this book you are down as a Rabbit, but some traditions call you a Hare (madder, larger ears) and others know you as a Cat. The Rabbit/Hare thing is understandable, but Cat? It's all about survival. You're both way up there on the "aaaah" scale of the kind, round-eyed furry cutitude that jams rational thought; cats have nine lives, and rabbits replicate so fast it hardly matters. You came a respectable fourth in the race to Buddha, because you like to mingle unnoticed with the crowd—it makes it easier to pick people's pockets.

What You See Ain't What You Get

Rabbit or Cat, you have the same agenda. You are on the planet to cut the best deal for yourself at the least possible expense and noise, and you have found that looking cute, sliding out of confrontations you cannot win, being economical with the truth, and having principles that bend like pretzels is the way forward. When you are feeling feline, you lie around being high-maintenance, and allow the rest of us to pay for the privilege of stroking you, or just basking in your purry warmth. If stronger-minded animals (usually Roosters) drop-kick you out of their lives, you always fall on your feet. If the Rabbit is strong in you, the rest of us have to

THE RABBIT

WATER RABBIT 1903, 1963

Flopsy Bunny, nearly always tired and emotional, awash in a sea of self-pity and remembrance of past slights—most of them imaginary, but many still useful for blackmailing purposes.

FIRE RABBIT 1927, 1987

Captainish sort of Rabbit, who bustles round putting up instructive notices signed "Rabbit," then gets into murderous rages when other animals ignore them.

METAL RABBIT 1951, 2011

Relentless RoboRabbit, whose empathy circuitry has blown, and whose software is entirely driven by black mood technology. Rabbitproof fences mean nothing to you.

remember that although you may look fluffy and adorable, you come from a long line of powerful trickster gods and will not hesitate to shaft us. Remember, Bugs Bunny's carrot empire was built on wit, trickery, guile, and routinely pretending to be something he wasn't.

Conspicuously sentimental and icky on the outside (clap your hands if you believe in fairies!), you are shrewd and heartless on the inside; but then in the Western zodiac you pick your way fastidiously along the fishy line that ties wet, devious, unreliable Pisces to ruthless, nitpicking, control-freak Virgo. Your convenience and comfort zone are all that matters—and if it means nuking a couple of villages crammed with sick orphans to keep it clear, you won't twitch a whisker, even if the dear white-haired old grandma looking after them is your own.

NOTORIOUS RABBITS

Rabbits hate to be the center of attention, but will be smugly pleased to know you have some world-beaters among the conmen, artists (Paul Klee), cute actors (Brad Pitt, Angelina Jolie), and people who want their real names to stay private (Sting).

Josef Stalin (b. December 21, 1879)

Who'd have thought it? One of the most ruthless dictators in history, responsible for the death of thousands of his own countrymen? Look at the M.O. Insignificant Georgian Iosif Vissarionovich Dzhugashvili (Stalin was a stage name) insinuated himself into power, capitalizing on the death of Lenin, and, once in charge, set about trying to make a world the way he wanted it. Other people's suffering and death meant nothing to him. Don't take Rabbits for granted.

Albert Einstein (b. March 14, 1879)

Another Rabbit that crept up on the world unawares and dropped a bombshell. Who was to know he was a genius (apart from his mom)? Einstein did not speak at all until he was three, got an indifferent degree, then worked for years as a clerk in a patent office. All the time he was secretly rearranging the world to fit his own special—if Relative—view.

Rabbit Mantra
I will survive

COMPANION ANIMALS

You also have an animal that sniffs around the hour of your birth (see pages 12–13 for details). According to Chinese tradition, the animal in charge of your birth hour gives you your social mask, the yang self that you present to the world.

(see pages 12–13 for details)

The Hour of the Rat

The Hour of the Snake

The Hour of the Ox

The Hour of the Dragon

The Hour of the Tiger

The Hour of the Rabbit

11:00 p.m.–12:59 a.m.
You find it even easier than other Rabbits to pretend to be warmer and cuddlier than you actually are, and so effortlessly charm more suckers out of their trust funds.

1:00–2:59 a.m.
Stubborn self-willed Rabbit who thinks Stalin was a fine role model and is proud to continue doing the work of one of Rabbitkind's finest.

9:00–10:59 a.m.
Moody, mysterious, enigmatic Rabbit, with a deeply significant, yet impenetrable agenda of your own. We remember you from *Donnie Darko*.

3:00–4:59 a.m.
Daring Rabbit who prefers to be counted as one of the Hares always racing, but never understands why Tortoise wins.

7:00–8:59 a.m.
Ruler of the salad patch; one commanding twitch of the whiskers and hench-bunnies rush to do your dirty work.

5:00–6:59 a.m.
Ah, *sensei*! You take no action because that would mean taking sides and you are in exquisite Zen balance; listen to the sound of one paw clapping.

Your native hour, the Hour of the Rabbit, runs from five o'clock to seven in the morning—a strategic time for ruthless plotting while everyone else is rubbing sleep from their eyes, and the favorite visiting hours of secret policemen everywhere.

THE RABBIT

The Hour of the Horse

The Hour of the Pig

The Hour of the Sheep

The Hour of the Dog

The Hour of the Monkey

The Hour of the Rooster

11:00 a.m.–12:59 p.m.
Bumptious, energetic Rabbit, more of a Hare; you love racing around the track with the greyhounds, for you always win. You don't understand why they won't let you place bets.

9:00–10:59 p.m.
Always ready to leap into the pie dish to provide a meal for friends, but then your inner Rabbit takes control and you allow yourself to be persuaded out again.

1:00–2:59 p.m.
Professional hedonist. Your Sheep majors in Sybaritic Studies, while your Rabbit persuades the rest of us to bankroll such gross self-indulgence.

7:00–8:59 p.m.
Gloomy Rabbit, convinced there will never be enough carrots to go around and that they are all full of pesticide residue anyway.

5:00–6:59 p.m.
Noisy, undiplomatic Rabbit; in Cat mode, you're Siamese. As Rabbits and Roosters don't get on, the noise is probably you expressing your inner turmoil.

3:00–4:59 p.m.
Brer Rabbit. Smart Monkey skills with top trickster DNA mean the rest of us should hand over our wallets now.

RABBIT IN LOVE

Rabbit or Cat, you only have to make sure your fur is sleek and glossy, then sit with your little paws tucked in and wait to be pampered. No one ever knows what you're feeling and you will never let on, because what you are feeling is nothing. Of course you don't wear your heart on your sleeve—you haven't actually got a heart. You come on sympathetic and supportive, and allow lovesick saps to make your fur damp with tears, but slide away skillfully when it looks as if there may be a messy scene, or you may actually have to lift a paw. That's why you always dump by email, text message, or mutual friend. Of course you don't do constancy; who knows when someone with more of the folding greenstuff, or a bigger milk jug, may come along?

Rabbit in Bed

Now you're talking. Despite your demure appearance, you are a total slut/sex machine between the sheets. (Remember, in Cat mode you are much like a Tiger, but more compact.) Lovers find you irresistible, especially your secret smile afterward. They think you want them for their minds, poor saps. Sex gives you enormous personal pleasure, but it need not necessarily be with someone else: why do you think a girl's best vibrating friend is called the Rabbit?

Hot Rabbits

Cary Grant: one of Golden Age Hollywood's most scrumptious leading men, charm on stilts, suave, urbane, the opposite of strong and silent; he wooed and won his women by talking to them, rather than dragging them by the hair. His movies were mostly wit and fizz and, like Bugs Bunny in another genre, he spent an inordinate amount of time dressed in women's clothing or pretending to be someone else. And he wasn't even American, or Cary Grant (until 1931 his name was Archibald Leach). *Rabbitissimo*.

And there's more ... Queen Victoria of England was a Class A Rabbit: too refined to find anything amusing; lived almost forever (the Rabbit is a symbol of longevity); passionately loved her Rabbit prince, Albert; and produced an unnecessary number of children.

THE RABBIT 兔

RABBIT DATE

You will only get a Rabbit date if you are rich, a
celeb (C list or above), an about-to-be-hot artist
or musician, or friends of any of the above, because
Rabbits (and Cats) are social mountaineers and just
adore the in-crowd. Assuming that your daddy owns
Westinghouse, that your experimental film is a cert
for Sundance, or that you are the third son of the
Duke of Poshampton, then Rabbit will kindly escort
you to the best restaurant in town, via a few stylish
boutiques where you have a charge card. You
discover when it is too late that this is at your
expense, and that you also seem to have bankrolled
their new business venture, even though you can't
remember signing a contract. If you are still useful,
they'll let you take them out again; before making a
fool of yourself, look deep into their eyes—there's
nothing there but hard little beads of glass.

MATING MISTAKES

Rabbit and Rat
Carbon rods will be needed as charm levels reach critical mass, but Rats do not have your staying power and keep remembering that you are sometimes a Cat.

Rabbit and Ox
Oxen are your natural prey, for they have money, but even an actor like you can't fake it as long as it takes for them to part with any.

Rabbit and Tiger
As a Cat, you feel obliged to roam with a brother; but as a Rabbit, you know that lockdown in the burrow is the smarter option.

Rabbit and Rabbit
How adorable do you two look? A chain of vomit buckets couldn't do it justice. I guess you're just in it for the chocolate-box royalties.

Rabbit and Dragon
Their breath scorches your fur and they are a bit vulgar, but it's worth abasing yourself, because Dragons move in all the best circles.

Rabbit and Snake
You give a good passionate stare, but they give better, and you are either swallowed whole or slowly squashed into oblivion.

Rabbit and Horse
They rush about too much and make huge piles of mess, but you try not to turn your nose up, for they might be a thoroughbred.

Rabbit and Sheep *
The Sheep's too clingy for your dispassionate taste, but the Goat makes you remember that your ancestors were pagan gods and witches' familiars.

Rabbit and Monkey
They smile to your face—and tell wicked lies about you behind your back. Who wants to be force-fed their own medicine?

Rabbit and Rooster
Distressingly noisy and bossy, and they always get up at dawn for the express purpose of squawking at you. Who needs it?

Rabbit and Dog
You cannot be serious? What usually happens when Dog meets Rabbit (or Cat)? Why aren't you up a tree or down a rabbit hole?

Rabbit and Pig
All right, they are affectionate, generous, kind, and keep you warm at night, but you wouldn't want to be seen out with them.

* For inscrutable Eastern reasons, the Sheep is also known as the Goat.

THE RABBIT

RABBIT AT WORK

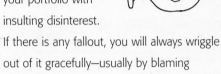

You're never out of a job because Rabbits always carry their lucky paw with them, and Cats always land on their feet. Whatever it is, you only work to your own agenda. Sometimes this coincides with the company's, and sometimes it doesn't—in which case you set about changing the company goals to suit yours. Boardroom brawling is far too undignified; you prefer bribery, insinuation, and trickery, and if this doesn't work, a stiletto between the ribs in the dark. In a new job, you always befriend everybody straight away, then watch and wait to see who will serve your purposes (it's a genuine mystery to you why the whole world doesn't dedicate itself to your comfort and advancement, but you have to be realistic). You cultivate the influential (not always the obvious candidates), and drop non-performers from your portfolio with insulting disinterest.

If there is any fallout, you will always wriggle out of it gracefully—usually by blaming someone else.

Office Politics

Macchiavelli (Ox) would be proud. You are so charming and discreet that everyone tells you their grubby secrets. And when you've got all that information, you set about subverting, ruining reputations with a whispering campaign that cannot be traced back to you, making and breaking alliances with a flick of your tail. At the first sign of trouble, you disappear down a rabbit hole that you made earlier, or are found snoozing innocently on top of your pristine paperwork.

TIME BANDIT	OFFICE INFECTOR	ASSET STRIPPER
You would never draw attention to yourself by being too late or too early, and are always at your work station when you should be, but not necessarily awake.	No chance! You limp in snuffling, and mew pitifully until sent home in a private ambulance, with two cute paramedics and the boss's compliments.	Most of the stuff at work is so ugly you wouldn't give it room in your house, but you fund essential personal business (florists, dry cleaners) with petty cash.

Rabbit Boss

You'd like to be, so that you can make sure things go your way, but you are not very good at it, because there is no crowd to hide behind if you mess up. So you hesitate and move too cautiously, and will not make a public decision, and Tigers or Dragons bounce in and seize power. You never confront if you can help it; but if you can't help it, you have perfected the tyranny of the weak maneuver, which means that you manipulate big, strong, shouty people into caving in to your demands because they look really bad and shameful bullying a dear, fluffy little thing like you.

Rabbit Slacker

At Rabbit Grade, you nibble away so industriously that no one likes to ask how exactly this is helping the company. If you are employed as a Cat, it is your job to doze in the sun all day looking beautiful—and you work really hard at it.

Rabbit 9–5er

You turn up regularly every day because it's warm, dry, and free. It's also the best way to blend indistinguishably into the workforce while you plot your way up the corporate ladder, and emerge—to everyone's surprise—at the second rung from the top.

Suitable Jobs for Rabbits

Actor   Gigolo   Politician   Trust fund baby   Chief advisor   Art thief

Mistress   Real estate agent   Double agent   Fence

RABBIT AT HOME

Rabbit Habitat

Rabbits are famously adaptable. As long as it is luxurious, private, and free, you will live anywhere. Few get invited to visit you because you prefer to be at their house, oozing charm and wrapping yourself around their champagne and oysters. Somewhere with a priest hole, curtained alcoves, secret passages, and unexpected staircases would suit you perfectly; however, you will make do with a luxury penthouse with only one private lift, but two or three defensible fire escapes.

Rabbit Neighbors

You have a cocktail party to work out who is where on the social scale, dropping the deadbeats, but scooping them up again with a smooth paw when you discover they are Connected. At night you nibble away at their fence boundaries. When they find out you are running an anti-government private militia cell, you will eliminate them without a thought; and when there is a dawn raid on their house, you snuggle deeper into your duvet. You just love collaborating with the authorities.

Feeding Habits

You're discriminating (what do you mean, "picky"?), which means you can only eat expensive organic while your kids live on cheeseburgers and aspartame. You suffer from instant, inexplicable allergies, usually to supermarket brand foods of any kind, but recover when presented with a menu from Spago handwritten by Wolfgang Puck. You always eat out—otherwise you'd have to cook and wash up. You know every maître d' in town.

THE RABBIT

Rabbit Roomie

You turn up in response to the ad for the pokiest room in the house, but within minutes are tucked up in your new roomie's luxury queen-size while they try to get a good night's sleep in the broom closet. They slave all day over a 10-course banquet for their boss and four other influential people; you join the table uninvited, charm the pants off the company, get the boss's private number, and, the following day, your roomie's job. The rent always gets paid, but never by you.

Rabbit Burrows

The perfect Rabbit warren must be luxurious, exclusive, and private, but with plenty of room for retail indulgence and gossip; Cats can do that, too.

* Wisteria Lane
* Megastar hotel
* Private island
* Bergdorf Goodman
* Canyon Ranch
* Palazzo Vecchio, Florence (lots of secret passages)

THE DRAGON

1904, 1916, 1928, 1940, 1952, 1964,
1976, 1988, 2000

FUTURE DRAGON: **2012**

Fixed element: **Wood**

Energy: **Yang**

Hour of the Dragon: **7:00–8:59 a.m.**

Month: **April**

Season: **Spring**

Direction: **East-southeast**

Chinese name: *Long*

The Way of the Overbearing Dragon

Arrogant, megalomaniac, critical, unpredictable, fanatical, tactless,
intimidating, dogmatic, dictatorial, pompous

WOOD DRAGON 1904, 1964

EARTH DRAGON 1928, 1988

Although your fixed element is Wood (*see page 15*), all five Dragons in the 60-year cycle scorch the earth at slightly different intensities, for each year is ruled by a different element.

A People's Dragon; you will graciously condescend to be pulled along on a flatbed float at any parade given in your honor, as long as the crowd is big enough.

You've got your fire breathing under control, and your flame burns hard and blue, a precision instrument you can use to forge the revolution—as long as you don't have to meet the peasants.

TEMPERAMENT

Get over yourself! You may be the fabulous luck bringer, the Guardian of Wealth and Power, and the totem of emperors in the East, but in the West you are the devourer of virgins and burner of crops, so we had to invent a whole heroic genre just to contain you. Still, it's better than being ignored. Being ignored is the worst thing that can happen to you—then you shrivel up and die. People wonder why a megastar like you only came fifth in the race to Buddha. Have they not heard of fashionably late? And how can you go anywhere without a security team in front to alert the paparazzi, and a band of fanatical worshippers behind?

Enter the Dragon

Your problem (sorry, challenge) is that you are not actually real. You are from a mythic dimension; your time–space continuum and ours don't quite synchronize, which is why you appear out of scale (tee-hee), larger than life, implausibly shiny, and totally misread the social map. It is imperative to get the rest of us to believe in you—otherwise you would disappear in a puff of smoke like the paper monster you are—so you burn up all your energies trying to bedazzle us. Your strength and will seem fabulous, like Superman's, but how are we to know you're not just a mild-mannered librarian back home with all the other fire breathers? You don't want us to find out, so you put on a constant show.

THE DRAGON

WATER DRAGON 1952, 2012	FIRE DRAGON 1916, 1976	METAL DRAGON 1940, 2000
You produce lots of noisy, hot steam rather than actual flames; a cooler head means that you think before you act, and the other dragons all sneer at you for slacking.	"I am the Emperor Tharg, Obey My Will." Melted enemy armor blocks the door of your cave, which is littered with the bones of virgins and underlings who questioned your orders.	Panzer Dragon, but not as scary and powerful as you think you are; the downside of a rigid chassis is that you can't dodge grenades that are lobbed in from odd angles.

Breathtakingly rude, in the way only the cripplingly rich or royal are (even though your daddy was a longshoreman), you do not mince words, suffer fools, apologize, or understand that these are all clichés that real people use ironically. You are gung-ho for the law (after all, your ancestors made it), but your task is to uphold it, not obey it; we should do as you say, not as you do, just like the low-grade worms back in your home realm. Slash and burn, shock and awe have always been your way. Trial by combat? Bring it on! Trial by jury? Far too slow.

It's no surprise that you storm along the line of fire that connects headbanger Aries with Libra the lawgiver in the Western zodiac. Always ready to forgive minor mistakes, you expect to be equally forgiven when you burn down a small city in a fit of pique (metaphorically, of course).

NOTORIOUS DRAGONS

It would be an insult to suggest any of you lack notoriety, fame, or even minor celebrity, so let's just say that among the many megastars, rocket scientists, monarchs, and tyrants of Dragonkind, here are a couple of incandescent examples.

Friedrich Nietzsche (b. October 15, 1844)
A bold Wood Dragon devoted to the big picture and hauling the rest of us up to the required standard, he invented the concept of superman, but was never credited by DC Comics. He cut to the chase by declaring God dead and undertaking a "reevaluation of all values," concluding that we are all driven by the will to power; he meant the will to power over our own base passions, but in true Dragon mode did not see how his words could be so easily misconstrued.

Salvador Dali (b. May 11, 1904)
Flamboyant showman with artistic flair; the modern artist everybody has heard of—even those who know nothing about art, but know what they like. Everyone thinks Dali's surreal landscapes are an expression of 20th-century dislocation; actually, they are scenes of his home dimension, painted from memory, to cheer himself up while trapped in this one.

Dragon Mantra
I rule!

THE DRAGON

COMPANION ANIMALS

You also have an animal that sniffs around the hour of your birth (see pages 12–13 for details). According to Chinese tradition, the animal in charge of your birth hour gives you your social mask, the yang self that you present to the world.

The Hour of the Rat

11:00 p.m.–12:59 a.m.
You love parading, but love even more knowing exactly how much people will pay to watch you doing it in all your luck-bringing splendor, and charge accordingly.

The Hour of the Snake

9:00–10:59 a.m.
Sinister, charming guile backed up by raw power. Probably a Bond villain; you blow it by stopping to show off and explain your world domination plan.

The Hour of the Ox

1:00–2:59 a.m.
Slow-burn Dragon, happy to sit quietly in the lair watching the treasure accumulate; if crossed, you will incinerate the entire state.

The Hour of the Dragon

7:00–8:59 a.m.
You'll have to set up a cult to create the total obedience, blind faith, and ceaseless adulation you need to stay alive.

The Hour of the Rabbit

5:00–6:59 a.m.
You suggest what you would like to happen, but never seriously expect a refusal, because that would mean you'd have to use your big fire stick.

The Hour of the Tiger

3:00–4:59 a.m.
Let's stand back and watch as doomed firefighters try to contain the explosion when you don't get your own way.

Your native hour, the Hour of the Dragon, rules between seven and nine in the morning, exactly the time to host a breakfast-time levee to show everyone how glorious you are and tell them what their day's agenda will be.

龍 THE DRAGON

The Hour of the Horse

11:00 a.m.–12:59 p.m.
Life and soul of whatever party you've crashed, an imperial wild child; you think nothing of gambling away your crown, and have to be shot by the palace guards for the sake of the dynasty.

The Hour of the Pig

9:00–10:59 p.m.
Heroic, chivalrous Dragon, who flames on the side of the Good Guys. Invariably toasted by evil Dragons, but the most popular beast in heraldry.

The Hour of the Sheep

1:00–2:59 p.m.
Can't believe you've got all these emeralds for just a bit of fire breathing; you spend happy hours designing flattering new settings for the clunkier pieces.

The Hour of the Dog

7:00–8:59 p.m.
Dragons and Dogs always fight, partly because Dog can't bear to see the giant hole Dragon is making in the ozone layer.

5:00–6:59 p.m.
Fairytale Dragon, fearless, proud, and noble; you believe in the stuff of legends and are always disappointed when life doesn't end happily ever after.

The Hour of the Monkey

3:00–4:59 p.m.
Huge power + huge guileful brain: you are probably one of those people who run the world, but don't look as if you do.

The Hour of the Rooster

DRAGON IN LOVE

You need immense amounts of adoration to stay alive, so you figure it's best to spread the load and are open to anyone who will put in the hours—often employing them in shifts. And because you are bursting with yang (even when your gender is yin) and a free spirit who loathes being tied down, you go for the harem option. Although you are impetuous, maddening, tactless, foul-tempered, and the opposite of intimate (extimate?), lovers of a certain temperament (mainly Goats) can't wait to immolate themselves in the white flame of your incandescence. You have no time for sulk-and-make-up, playful lovers' tiffs, and tearful muttering over cigarettes that bear a lipstick's traces. You prefer a straight fight, and if they leave, you won't chase them.

Dragon in Bed

You think you are the Great Seducer and a sexual artist, but you are clumsy and ignore all the subtle details that make lovers faint with lust. On the other hand, you are a passionate, energetic, and determined perfectionist, and if you don't get it right the first time, you will keep at it until you get a result—even if this means continuing into office hours or carrying on after your partner has gone home. You get through rather a lot of beds.

Hot Dragons

Although no great beauty, Mae West ("Why don't you come up sometime, and see me?") was a triumph of self-belief, and made a long and successful career out of showing off and sex. Her first controversial play, which she wrote and starred in, was called *Sex* (no subtlety there, then), and for her breakthrough film, *She Done Him Wrong* (1933), she hand-picked Cary Grant as her leading man. Still at it in 1978, when she made *Sextette* at 85. Don't mess with Lady Dragons.

And there's more … According to Dragons, all of you are incandescent and most of you are stars; the rest of us can choose from testosterone-laden alpha males (James Cagney, Tom Jones, and Russell Crowe) or beautiful alpha screen goddesses (Julie Christie, Faye Dunaway, and Marlene Dietrich).

龍 THE DRAGON

DRAGON DATE

Dragons don't do rainchecks; if they invite you on a date, you go. Don't bother explaining about a previous engagement, because they will already have canceled it for you and cleared your diary for the next few weeks. Your dying grandmother will just have to wait. The good news is that it won't be an intimate one-on-one. The night has a thousand eyes, and Dragons want every one of those eyes locked onto them. The stretch limo/Ferrari Testarossa will pick you up promptly and whisk you to this week's hottest showbiz watering hole, where you are allowed to spend the evening watching Dragon show off, hog the karaoke, kick in the slot machines that refuse to pay out, drink 17 tequila slammers in a row for a bet, and punch out the bar staff for serving them too slowly. It'll be great. If you don't want them to call back, you will have to leave the planet for a while.

MATING MISTAKES

Dragon and Rat

You think they love you for your flaming passion; they are waiting for the post-coital snooze, so that they can get at the treasure hoard you sleep on.

Dragon and Ox

You see a flaming symbolic beacon; they see a barbecue. You see castles in the clouds; they bring an umbrella. You say love apple; they say tomato.

Dragon and Tiger

An eyeball-to-eyeball confrontation about who drives, where you are going, and whether you take their chopper or your jumpjet means you're not going anywhere.

Dragon and Rabbit

They give really great adoring, but in return you have to give them backstage passes so that they can outclass their friends.

Dragon and Dragon

You know two Dragons from legend space cannot occupy the same coordinates in real space; why do you keep on trying to do so?

Dragon and Snake

They love to wind their bodies sinuously around yours, but that is because you provide a cheaper heating system in winter.

Dragon and Horse

They are handsome, self-centered, and demanding; you are handsome, demanding, and self-centered. Just how is this going to work?

Dragon and Sheep

They think that coming on dainty, capricious, and winsome will inflame you; they've forgotten your legendary response to twittering girlies.

Dragon and Monkey

They know to the syllable how much outrageous flattery it takes to make you roll over on your back and open your wallet.

Dragon and Rooster

War of the wardrobes; neither of you will ever leave the house for fear of being outdazzled by the other, and you steal each other's shirts.

Dragon and Dog

Unimpressed by your show-stopping numbers, because they can sniff out that you're not from around these parts.

Dragon and Pig

Roast pork! Pig will do anything for you, but you can't have a serious liaison with the staff. If only they didn't taste so good.

DRAGON AT WORK

In your home dimension, routine work and maintenance are carried out by insignificant trolls, while you glitter and shine on a pile of gold and flirt only with heroes, gods, and royalty. You have never really got a grip on how it works here; nor do you want to, because it all seems so petty and grubby. You are doing your best to follow the mythic imperative, offering yourself up as a beacon to the little people; it's just that it looks like insatiable ambition to the rest of us. You say initiator, we say fire starter. Your ideas are audacious and grandiose, but you leave the detail to middle management and bean counters—which would be fine except that you regularly fire them all in outbursts of temper, and smash with one lash of your tail the prototype that the tech team has spent six painstaking months putting together.

Because you are an emperor, you spurn the greasy pole and the career ladder and will not mingle socially with the lower orders (catch you dancing with the staff at the office party!). Your people skills are appalling—how many courses have you been sent on now?—because you cannot read body language and see others only as stereotypes, lackeys, or lunch.

Office Politics

You disdain gossip because you don't know how to do it, and see no reason to flatter or cajole. The swirl of plots and insurrections that percolates through any corporation means nothing to you as you surge forward on wings of chutzpah, with no regard for whoever gets caught in the downdraft—a large, slow-moving target for the cunning.

TIME BANDIT	OFFICE INFECTOR	ASSET STRIPPER
You will turn up, and leave, when it's convenient for you. If it's not convenient for everybody else, tough! They are lucky to get you at all.	You are rarely ill, though often on crutches; there are not enough wild horses in the world to prevent you showing up, even if you are clinically dead.	The repair bills for the printers, copiers, and so on that you trash are astronomical, as are the replacement costs for the scorch marks on the ceiling.

Dragon Boss

This is the safest place for you, as long as there is a dedicated, fireproof management team between you and the workforce. Everybody wants the kind of luck and energy you generate, but your oppressive day-to-day presence, volcanic temper, and regular incineration of the boardroom (with the Board still in it) are a high price to pay.

Dragon Slacker

If only; you party every night, yet still bounce into the office every day, thermostat on high, ready to irritate, annoy, contradict, and confront your colleagues, who are all feeling a bit fragile. You don't understand the subtle art of looking busy while doing nothing, because you are always doing something—even if it does mean that the emergency services have to be called out.

Dragon 9–5er

Bad news for your fellow grunts. Because you cannot endure routine and won't take orders from anyone, you do what you want, regardless of the consequences or how deep a pile of dragon doo-doo it lands others in. "A foolish consistency is the hobgoblin of the tiny mind," you thunder, as security clears your workstation and escorts you off the premises.

Suitable Jobs for Dragons

Cult leader

Emperor/empress of the Cosmos

Star (rock, movie, mega)

Overlord

Savior of the World

Destroyer of the World

Mad inventor

DRAGON AT HOME

Dragon Habitat

In legend you dwell in underwater caverns, where you doze all day on piles of emeralds, gold, and the skulls of heroes. This is hard to replicate here in Reality, but you do your best with cavernous apartments converted from old locomotive sheds, crumbling Venetian palazzi, decayed antebellum mansions. Scale is all: you need a big turning circle. Loud and vulgar with lots of gold is what you like, plus a magnificent lighting system to show off your best side.

Dragon Neighbors

You never have trouble with the neighbors, as long as they don't bother you; they are delightful little people. You are always ready to lead the neighborhood watch into battle against bureaucracy and have single-handedly increased sectarian unrest in your patch by 200 percent. If your neighbors make too much noise, you burn down their shed as a reprimand. If they complain about your noise, you roar at them to show what real noise is. They usually move away after that.

Feeding Habits

Back in the home dimension you don't do eating —you do devouring, and your meal is usually alive and protesting. Here, you pass as a hearty eater and are very popular with Pig moms, who always overcater. There is only one way to cook, and that is to barbecue. You never waste eating time looking for intimate, candlelit cafés; you want the window table in big, bright celebrity restaurants: preferably ones with a waiting list, solid gold flatware, and a Dragons-only door policy.

Dragon Roomie

Few people resist when you announce you are moving in, although the more sensible ones take out extra insurance and install more smoke alarms. Luckily, you are not at home often because you are out partying or righting wrongs, but when you do come back (usually at 4 a.m.), you bring the party with you. Of course you don't do chores—not when there's a whole houseful of less important people to do them for you; you pay your way once a year, usually in doubloons or gold bricks.

Dragon Dimensions

You can never quite recreate home, but you are drawn to places that have space, opulence, and glamour. You love Vegas.

* Hollywood Bowl
* Sherwood Forest
* Versailles
* Taj Mahal
* The White House
* The Ritz
* Atlantis
* The Forbidden City, Beijing

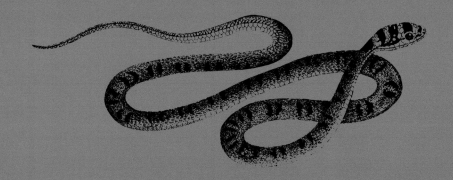

THE SNAKE

1905, 1917, 1929, 1941, 1953, 1965,
1977, 1989, 2001

FUTURE SNAKE: **2013**

Fixed element: **Fire**

Energy: **Yin**

Hour of the Snake: **9:00–10:59 a.m.**

Month: **May**

Season: **Spring**

Direction: **South-southeast**

Chinese name: *She*

The Way of the Slithering Snake

Sly, sinister, possessive, jealous, vindictive, vicious, wily,
superstitious, sophisticated, intense, suspicious, lazy,
demanding, distrustful, evasive

IN YOUR ELEMENT

Although your fixed element is Fire (*see page 15*), all five snakes in the 60-year cycle slough off their dead selves in different ways, for each year is ruled by a different element.

WOOD SNAKE 1905, 1965

Seductive guru with expensive tastes; worshippers get to purify themselves by imagining no possessions; you get to enrich yourself with a fleet of Rolls-Royces and a platinum card.

EARTH SNAKE 1929, 1989

Smooth, smart, enigmatic, secretive, etc., yet somehow dull; more of a wyrm than a viper. (A wyrm is a large, possibly mythical, eel-like reptile with pretensions to dragonhood.)

TEMPERAMENT

For most of us, however hard we try to rise above it, the snake puts the fear of God into us, even if it's just a harmless grass snake. Only a maniac would approach a snake without a forked stick and a worried expression. And don't you Snakes just love that? In the East they go on about your mystery, inscrutability, wisdom, and karmic overload, but they also call you a "dragon without wings," which means that all that energy and power turns inward and drives impulses so deep that not even you know about them. You came sixth in the race to Buddha—not keen and obvious, but not so late that no one thinks you're a serious contender.

Snake in the Grass

Sophisticated, cool, languid, self-possessed, and unfathomable, you make the rest of us feel klutzy, overdressed, overheated, unsubtle, and grimy, with too many ugly sticky-out bits. You prefer to lie in elegant coils at the bottom of your basket, waiting for just the right moment to execute a venomous surgical strike; it may look as if you're asleep, but we can't be certain. You see no reason for idle banter, empty chatter, or communication of any kind, unless it is the one-way beam of your hooded eyes as you bend the weak to your will. Don't forget that in the Western zodiac you slither along the celestial umbilical cord that links unstoppable Taurus with relentless Scorpio.

THE SNAKE

WATER SNAKE 1953, 2013

Wily serpent, with your mind coiled tightly round the big picture; you harbor grudges for a lifetime, but will wait until just the right moment to sink in the fangs or shake the rattle.

FIRE SNAKE 1917, 1977

Power-crazed solipsist, with an insatiable desire for unlimited fame, wealth, and power, which you plan to share with no one else; everybody needs somebody, but you don't.

METAL SNAKE 1941, 2001

Scheming loner who plays to win at all costs; you often fail, because you think everyone else is fueled by the same deep, dark motives as you are, and so you totally misread the situation.

Being ruthless, tenacious, possessive, and demanding, you have never apologized or explained; when angered, you simply follow the Way of the Boa and squeeze your enemies until they squeal, or stare icily at them until they slash their own wrists. And when you have enslaved the rest of us (mainly the Piggies) and have sucked out all the marrow from our dull little animal minds, you discard us, for one of your many skills is the ability to slough off old, unwanted skin, friends, family, and workmates, and slither off to a new life. Neither you nor we have forgotten that when the Prince of Darkness wanted to lure Adam and Eve into naughtiness, he undulated through the Garden of Eden dressed as a serpent, switched on his hypnotic gaze, and spoke softly with forked tongue; what a major-league role model for Snakes everywhere.

NOTORIOUS SNAKES

An alarming number of enigmatic, silent, scary persons belong to the Snake sect, including Lord Voldemort, Potter nemesis and heir to Salazar Slytherin. Think Howard Hughes, Garbo, E. A. Poe. If that sounds a bit Gothick, consider these two.

THE SNAKE

Mao Zedong (b. December 26, 1893)
No one saw this Snake coming, sliding out of the rice fields of an obscure peasant village in Hunan province to lead the largest country in the world. Convinced of his destiny (though few others were) from the age of 13, Mao plotted and wriggled his way to the top, silently enduring great hardship and jettisoning inconvenient loved ones on the way. Once there, he held on to power by plots and counterplots, suspicion, whispers, and the ability to scare people witless.

Elizabeth I of England (b. September 7, 1533)
The *femme fatale* (literally, if you were the Earl of Essex) who proved that a "weak and feeble" woman could stay on longer (on the throne, that is) and do more for the country than anyone with a Y chromosome. Everyone fell in love with her—and she was wise enough to keep them all hanging on until she got what she wanted (the New World).

Snake Mantra
Look into my eyes

COMPANION ANIMALS

You also have an animal that sniffs around the hour of your birth (see pages 12–13 for details). According to Chinese tradition, the animal in charge of your birth hour gives you your social mask, the yang self that you present to the world.

The Hour of the Rat

11:00 p.m.–12:59 a.m.
Your outer Snake gives you a suave, sophisticated sheen so that you can slide silently into higher social classes for some high-class hustling above your station.

The Hour of the Snake

9:00–10:59 a.m.
Twisty double helix of hooded glamorous menace; dealing with you is like being caught between Naga and Nagini, the twin Cobra gods of Hinduism.

The Hour of the Ox

1:00–2:59 a.m.
Constrictor style suits you; Ox gives you extra strength and stamina to squeeze and squeeze until you've got every last drop from your victim.

The Hour of the Dragon

7:00–8:59 a.m.
You rule, but wisely pack your own poison fangs, so don't need to rely on henchmen to see off your enemies.

The Hour of the Tiger

3:00–4:59 a.m.
Blazing gold and black stripes and Tiggerish crashing about in the undergrowth are no help in subtle undercover ops.

The Hour of the Rabbit

5:00–6:59 a.m.
You look cute and adorable in the pet store, and it's only when people get home and open the basket that they notice your flickering forked tongue.

Your native hour, the Hour of the Snake, stretches luxuriously between nine and eleven in the morning, because you don't do early and prefer to meet your enemies in broad daylight when they least expect it.

THE SNAKE

The Hour of the Horse

The Hour of the Pig

The Hour of the Sheep

11:00 a.m.–12:59 p.m.
Cheerful little trouser snake, you love zipping up and down life's ladders, but are lacking in enigma. You've got fangs, but they're not poisonous, although you bite when you want.

9:00–10:59 p.m.
Pigs and Snakes play on opposite teams. Pigs are obvious and appeasing, Snakes are subtle and picky. Best stay coiled up in bed; at least you both love sex.

1:00–2:59 p.m.
Your outer Sheep likes beautiful, expensive things; your inner Snake knows how to get them. Most people think those two Picassos on your wall are prints.

7:00–8:59 p.m.
Rattled snake; you fret silently within, tie yourself in inextricable knots, then sulk when you can't digest your food.

5:00–6:59 p.m.
You will never let anyone forget that you are the top Aztec god, Quetzalcoatl, the plumed serpent. Being subtle is not the only way to win.

3:00–4:59 p.m.
You bring your own snake charmer and work the crowd together, bedazzling the stupid gullible and beguiling the stupid rich.

The Hour of the Dog

The Hour of the Monkey

The Hour of the Rooster

SNAKE IN LOVE

Passionate, seductive, possessive, and jealous, you are exhausting, yet irresistible (except to the Tiger, who can't see what all the fuss is about). It takes you 45 seconds max. to ensnare a victim, and once you have got the poor sap, you never let go. You will know they are cheating before they do, and your vengeance will be exquisite; we are talking more than just stitching week-old shrimp into the drape linings here. You'll be there on their wedding night, all in black, sliding the Cartier stiletto into their heart. This does not mean you do not play away yourself; au contraire, there is nothing you like better than complicating your love life with dangerous liaisons. High-maintenance mistressing is a great career choice for Snakes of all genders.

Snake in Bed

Snakes love being in bed, especially when they shouldn't be, and this will be long, slow, and sensual, probably tantric, and usually in the afternoon. What's the problem, you cry? Well, bladder control for a start; and dehydration. And Snakes are very Demanding—if you know what I mean. If you please them, they will lock you up as their eternal lust slave; if you can't keep up, they'll sneer at you.

Hot Snakes

Who else could it be but Giacomo Casanova, the official Great Lover of the Western World? He had a head start, being born in wicked Venice to actor parents, but topped that by getting expelled from school for scandalous conduct (what can he have done to outrage the Sodom and Gomorrah of 18th-century Europe?), and imprisoned for Freemasonry and dabbling in the Black Arts. How he fitted the seducing in, no one knows.

And there's more ... Snakes have always cut swathes through the rest of the zoo (didn't you, JFK, Picasso?) and the female is more drop-dead gorgeous than the male (Princess Grace Kelly, First Lady Jackie O, Elf-queen Liv Tyler).

蛇 THE SNAKE

SNAKE DATE

Don't worry, you are in no danger of a Snake date
if you aren't seriously loaded (or so talented that
you soon will be), because Snakes do not do
slackers or the poor. Nor will you have any choice
in the matter: a little hypnotism, a discreetly
sensual slither, a flicker of the tongue, and there
you are outside Tiffany's wondering anxiously
whether Paloma Picasso diamond earrings are
not too cheap for a first-date offering. You go
somewhere luxurious, warm, private, and dark, so
that you can't see other people's expressions of
compassion. Snake will murmur slowly and softly,
stare into your eyes, and ply you with black wine.
Avoid greeting exes or old friends, otherwise Snake
will have them dealt with in a dark alley. Snake will
then take you back to their place in a limo with
black windows, and no one will see you again.

MATING MISTAKES

Snake and Rat

If you find Rat is playing away, you devour them as a light post-coital lunch; they won't mind as long as you wash them down with a really good Shiraz.

Snake and Ox

You thought you did a pretty mean Jealous and Possessive, but—stuck fast here under the Ox hoof—you realize that you are a mere Brownbelt, they are a Master.

Snake and Tiger

Your liaisons will be really *dangereuses* if Tiger finds out about them; you may lose your skin earlier than you had planned.

Snake and Rabbit

You can see right through Rabbit's fluffiness to the little ice-cube heart, but are too lazy to generate enough passion to melt it.

Snake and Dragon

Chinese astrological lore says that the Dragon loves you; well (yawn!), where's the challenge in that? You like live meat.

Snake and Snake

You will probably both end up on Death Row after your pact to poison each other's partners and slither away together has been discovered.

Snake and Horse

By the time you've got going with the dreamy, hypnotic seduction bit, Horse has come, had a rubdown, and gone again.

Snake and Sheep

You dismiss it as just another easy conquest, then you find bits of wool stuck to your skin, your credit card maxed out, and a bunny boiling on the hob.

Snake and Monkey

Monkey thinks it's fun to tie you in knots, then use you to swing around the jungle. You squeeze them to death in the night.

Snake and Rooster

Rooster overestimates how far a fine set of feathers and a perfectly pitched crow will impress you. You don't do obvious.

Snake and Dog

Look, you demanded total commitment and loyalty because that is part of your game. Now you have a 24/7 faithful friend. Be careful what you wish for.

Snake and Pig

Pig's friends try to tear them away, but it is no good, you have them immobilized and their heart on toast. It's lazy fun to make them watch while you misbehave.

SNAKE AT WORK

You must have money, power, and beautiful things. How to get them, at minimum cost to yourself? You are intelligent, so you know you have to work for these things, but the real challenge is to get them without breaking sweat. As long as it is indoors, somewhere warm, and does not involve unpleasant physical activity, you can do almost anything—but it's best to stick to what you know, which is lying very still and making lightning surgical strikes. So you're a natural for a job in the money market: you understand how cash flows in sinuous twists (rather like you do) and can follow it very easily, even while apparently asleep in a nest of silk cushions. Full of guile, cunning, and persistence, you are in constant plot-and-scheme mode, and will slither to the top in any profession that does not involve heavy lifting. You do this by relentlessly eliminating rivals and seducing the unworldly into doing that bit of building your empire that involves actual building; loyal suckers who've helped you make it should not even dream of rewards. Ultra-lazy Snakes short-circuit the work thing by marrying money; you can do this with ease, because all Snakes are top *femmes fatales*, whether or not they are *femmes*.

Office Politics

You rule—it comes naturally to you. You distrust everybody, and are always on your guard, especially when people don't think you are. You know where the bodies are buried, and never leave a score unsettled, but always rattle your enemies by making them wait for the payback.

TIME BANDIT	OFFICE INFECTOR	ASSET STRIPPER
Your time is your own, but everyone is certain you are somewhere in the building, because you always leave your spare skin draped over the chair.	A Snake sick note is rare—you would not want to miss a day, because other people might start up intrigues without you. So you infect others? So what!	Paperclip rustling? Photocopier abuse? Oh, please. You prefer to intercept funds traveling between fat-cat accounts and let them rest in yours for a while.

Snake Boss

You are the real king of the jungle, whatever that Leo oaf from the West says. You can quell any boardroom rebellion or a shopfloor riot with one lift of an eyebrow, and never waste energy raising your voice: why shout when you can hiss? Your workforce is terrified of you, because they never know when you will strike and will do anything you say, including lemming-leaping from the 44th floor.

Snake Slacker

To the unwary and naïve, you appear to be a champion slacker, because you don't move around much and spend a lot of time with your eyes closed. They are wrong! Inside that sleek, immobile exterior you are scheming your tenth move ahead of the game. And if it turns out that you are a real slacker, you have such a poisonous tongue that no one would dare say so to your face.

Snake 9–5er

Not a good look. Your unblinking stare unnerves bosses, who suspect you of dumb insolence (they are right). You will not be told, and always prefer to follow your own judgment rather than any ridiculous orders from someone way dumber than you (that's everyone then). If they knew of a safe way to fire you, they would.

Suitable Jobs for Snakes

Inquisitor

Tax lawyer

Assassin

Corporate raider

Politician

SNAKE AT HOME

Snake Habitat

Your needs are few: just a discreet bijou mansion (with real *bijoux*) that is grander than anyone else's, with top-of-the-line central heating, sofas, daybeds, loungers, and chaises longues in every room, so there is always somewhere to lie down gracefully when you need to—plus maybe one of those carpeted conversation pits to coil up in. Outside is not really you, although a lush conservatory, full of languid plants to hide behind, is a paradise for plots and whispers.

Snake Neighbors

You have no interest in anyone else's tedious little life, and no intention of giving anything away about your own exciting, dangerous one. You are secretive and suspicious and paranoid, so you assume the neighbors are fugitives from the IRS, or bigamists, just because you are (possibly). If you catch them crossing the invisible property line that only you know about, you will slowly crush their spirit and freeze them out of the neighborhood.

Feeding Habits

In public, fastidious nibbling of gastronomic delights on someone else's account is your style; you always leave a lot on your plate, allegedly because of your famously fragile digestion, but really because you like to make other diners feel fat. In private, you eat large animals whole, have an ongoing affair with the pizza delivery boy, and feed a shamefully uncool cake habit, which you hope no one knows about. They do now.

蛇 THE SNAKE

Snake Roomie

No one can remember how you insinuated yourself into the household, but fortunately you rarely come out of your room. As a philosopher, you believe that objects only exist in platonic space and are therefore available to everyone—so what's yours is yours, and what's everybody else's is also yours. You spit on lesser minds that cannot grasp this. The bathroom is littered with old skins you slough off, but no one mentions this, or the chores you never do. Someone else pays your rent.

Snake Nests

Snakes will only consent to live where there is warmth, darkness, luxury, privacy, and discreet, unbribable staff, trained in the martial arts. What about:

* Swiss bank vault
* Botanical gardens
* Boutique hotel
* Private club
* Tutankhamun's burial chamber
* Cartier's, Tiffany's, Bulgari's

THE HORSE

1906, 1918, 1930, 1942, 1954, 1966,
1978, 1990, 2002

FUTURE HORSE: **2014**

Fixed element:	**Fire**
Energy:	**Yang**
Hour of the Horse:	**11:00 a.m.–12:59 p.m.**
Month:	**June**
Season:	**Summer**
Direction:	**South**
Chinese name:	*Ma*

The Way of the Bolting Horse

Fickle, inconsistent, excitable, impatient, unruly, stubborn, shifty,
volatile, self-centered, irresponsible, rash,
unpredictable, erratic, inconsiderate

Although your fixed element is Fire (*see page 15*), all five Horses in the 60-year cycle kick down their stable doors in a different manner, for each year is ruled by a different element.

Being name-checked at Troy and hanging with Achilles, Odysseus, and the crew obliges you to be a tad more disciplined than the rest of the stable, but there's no need to be so smug.

Carthorse—serviceable but ploddish, and there are not enough sticks and carrots in the world to make you shift your great hooves if anyone tries to drive you a new way home.

TEMPERAMENT

In the West, horses can do little wrong *(they are our four-legged friends, they save the farm, they even have their own TV shows), so you're probably feeling pretty smug right now. Whoa there, compadre! Eastern astrologers have a rather better understanding of your self-centered, skittish, unreliable form, and have you tethered as overambitious, overcompetitive, and oversexed. In the race to Buddha, the Horse came in seventh; given the pathetic state of the competition, surely this calls for a Stewards' Inquiry? Did the syndicate pay you to throw the race, or did you have a complicated, yet high-yielding side bet?*

Dark Horse

You see yourself as a gorgeous, glossy thoroughbred, romping home with the Kentucky Derby between your teeth; or maybe as Bucephalus, Alexander the Great's supercharger; or as one of those saddle-free horses that get so much advertising work. The words "nag," "cat food," and "glue factory" are not part of your vocabulary, for you are pathologically vain—all that mane tossing just to show the rest of us you're worth it.

High profile? There's no escaping you. Not only are you the hot-blooded, unbridled playboy of the Chinese zodiac, you are also the tedious life and soul of the Western zodiac, as the equine half of Sagittarius the centaur. In the West the human part of the

THE HORSE

WATER HORSE 1942, 2002

Bold, smart, and shiny, but punters soon learn that you are unreliable in the field, because you are powered by random outbursts of energy and often run off the course completely.

FIRE HORSE 1906, 1966

Hot favorite, but rogue. You always throw your rider and the race, as you are easily distracted by bright lights; breathtaking over the flat, but bored by hurdles, and no staying power.

METAL HORSE 1930, 1990

Irresponsible bolter, one of the wild horses that don't seem to be able to drag anybody away from anything, so they run away themselves before they have to do any paperwork.

centaur adds restraint, but in the East you are all horse, with little sense, overflowing with yang and brimming with personality, so the rest of us have to go and lie down for a bit after a session with you. Not much will stop you talking, and it's always a relief when you dash off to investigate pastures new (in the Western zodiac you gallop along the inside straight between motor-mouth Gemini and attention-deficit Sagittarius).

You insist on giving advice (straight from the horse's mouth, and via a megaphone to a large crowd), but whinny contemptuously if anyone else offers you hints in return. If you can't do things your way—at once—you stamp your hooves and trample any opposition into the mud. Every Eastern astrologer observes that the Horse always leaves the home stable when young, but my guess is you are thrown out before you kick the place down.

NOTORIOUS HORSES

Of course, you are a rugged individualist, but you can't help feeling a frisson of herd pleasure when you see the number of freedom fighters, astronauts, rebels, evangelists, rock stars, tyrants, and charismatic politicians who run with you.

THE HORSE

Genghis Khan (b. May 5, 1162—probably)

I am taking a chance here, as Genghis (real name Borjigin Temujin) might also have been born in 1155 (Rabbit) or 1167 (Pig), but I am not convinced that someone who put together the largest land empire ever known (from China to the Danube), by sheer personal energy, could be anything but a Horse. Plus, the entire empire was made possible by horsepower, as Ghenghis's Mongol horde galloped everywhere on small, indomitable ponies. I rest my case.

James Dean (b. February 8, 1931)

Poster boy for sexy young rebels everywhere, Dean enjoyed a short but intense career as a megastar from 1952 until his completely avoidable death three years later. A hot-headed, live-fast-die-young Metal Horse, who followed the mythic imperative and died at the wheel of his own car after continuous boring warnings not to drive so fast.

Horse Mantra

I want to break free

COMPANION ANIMALS

You also have an animal that sniffs around the hour of your birth (see pages 12–13 for details). According to Chinese tradition, the animal in charge of your birth hour gives you your social mask, the yang self that you present to the world.

The Hour of the Rat

11:00 p.m.–12:59 a.m.
Although normally you find each other difficult, you collaborate to set up a lucrative betting scam: you make the running and your outer Rat fleeces the punters.

The Hour of the Snake

9:00–10:59 a.m.
You don't need to tire yourself out with all that running to win a race; simply nobble the favorite, bet with the syndicate on every other horse, *et voilà*.

The Hour of the Ox

1:00–2:59 a.m.
You look like a serious contender with lots of solid form; everyone bets the farm on you, you get all the way round, then stubbornly refuse the last fence.

The Hour of the Dragon

7:00–8:59 a.m.
Supercharger. It's imperative you win, so don't stop, even when you've streaked past the post and out into open country.

The Hour of the Rabbit

5:00–6:59 a.m.
At the starting post you look too refined to run; that's to distract from your huge, powerful thigh muscles, which produce killer bursts of speed when least expected.

The Hour of the Tiger

3:00–4:59 a.m.
Stunt horse: raw Tiger energy made to pay off by Horse's ability to turn on a dime. Was one of your grandfathers in *Ben Hur*?

Your native hour, the Hour of the Horse, runs between eleven and one o'clock and covers midday: the best the day's going to get, when everything seems possible, all bets look good, and you're convinced you can finish that report by lunchtime.

THE HORSE

The Hour of the Horse

The Hour of the Pig

The Hour of the Sheep

The Hour of the Dog

The Hour of the Monkey

The Hour of the Rooster

11:00 a.m.–12:59 p.m.
Headstrong, frisky pure breed, insufferably sure of your own glossy glory, and always liable to bolt; you'd be put down if you weren't carrying so many people's shirts on your back.

9:00–10:59 p.m.
Dull, complacent plodder with no winning streak; always get the bacon home, but not with any speed or style; much livelier after a week at the stud farm.

1:00–2:59 p.m.
Racing's a bit sweaty, so you concentrate on winning the Best Turned Out award, by persuading your owner to employ the finest grooms money can buy.

7:00–8:59 p.m.
Few people ride out with you more than once, because you shy at unexpected objects and throw your rider if they pull to the right.

5:00–6:59 p.m.
Dressage is your favorite event, because only clever horses can do it; plus you like anything that means wearing plumes: the circus, a military parade, funerals …

3:00–4:59 p.m.
Pony express. You give signed receipts for everyone's letters, pay checks, etc., gallop off into the dusty distance, and are never seen again.

HORSE IN LOVE

Love is the drug for you, isn't it? You can't get enough of it, and it doesn't really matter about the supplier—love the one you're with, you snort; it saves so much time. Like all drugs, love has its downside, and for you this is distraction from your primary purpose of galloping everywhere at once, very fast. Love objects expect you to spend time and attention on them, when there is so much more to do, and they tend to fire you when you don't deliver. So your heart is broken regularly, but as it's only made of straw, it's easily mended. And you find it more time-efficient to run a string of lovers simultaneously, so they can all break your heart at once and you can get over it and move on. Commitment? You would do anything for love—but you won't do that.

Horse in Bed

Lucky you! What you lack in looks, you make up for in raw sexual magnetism, so rolling around in the hay is always an option. Depending on your Horse type, you either come and go in a heated rush (all thrusts of speed, but no staying power) or you plod along dependably. And you always get your partner home in the end, even though the slow motion may have rocked them to sleep.

Hot Horses

Steve McQueen, the unreconstructed Metal stallion of the stable; he made women go all funny and throw feminist principles out of the window, and men want to be him. A serial bolter in real life, his greatest screen moment was *The Great Escape* (what else?), but the love of his life was his racing car.

And there's more … All those lean, laconic, tall-in-the-saddle guys (Clint Eastwood, Harrison Ford, Denzel Washington, Sean Connery) or long-legged girls (Cindy Crawford) you'd love to be, if only you weren't a mouthy little pit pony.

THE HORSE

HORSE DATE

Log your ICE (In Case of Emergency) number into your cellphone, check how far it is to the nearest trauma unit, then try to enjoy yourself. Horse dates always involve action—and not just the obvious kind. However besotted with you they are, no Horse is going to pass up the chance to para-ski with great white sharks for a mere date, so you will have to go along. And you'd think that after you'd been lashed together for a tandem sky jump, tumbling through the void in close embrace, they'd remember your name, but don't count on it. Horses are passionate when they're with you, but don't do oppressive. They'll call, but if you're not available, then your roomie will be. And they'll disappear for years, then mosey back into town— and your life—and act as if they saw you only yesterday. And you'll let them.

MATING MISTAKES

Horse and Rat
After a night of hot, straw-igniting passion, you discover that they've emptied your feed bins, and run away with the takings from the circus double-act you worked together.

Horse and Ox
When you two are yoked together, the plow keeps going around in circles, because you move much faster than they do.

Horse and Tiger
Painless—you ping off a text message explaining how you need more space; they do the same. Neither of you reads them.

Horse and Rabbit
They seemed so sweet; then came the incessant grooming and the picking out of tasteful neckties to make you look more acceptable. Surely the judge will understand?

Horse and Dragon
They have imperial longings, and insist that you play Roman chariot games. Guess who always ends up pulling the chariot.

Horse and Snake
They whisper that they can help you win the Big Race, then hobble you by winding themselves around your legs so that you can't run anywhere.

Horse and Horse
Prom queen and top jock; won't everyone be surprised when you file for divorce after six months, citing irreconcilable similarities.

Horse and Sheep
They look at you adoringly, but that is because they are calculating how much you'll net them at the horse fair.

Horse and Monkey
It will all be over when you catch them selling intimate, straight-from-the-stable information about your form and stamina to the National Enquirer and cable TV.

Horse and Rooster
Rooster rides on your back (they love jockey silks), constantly squawking critical advice and giving a fence-by-fence analysis of the races you have already run and won.

Horse and Dog
Of course horses and hounds go together, but you have to learn that this does not apply if you are a plow-horse and they are a teacup chihuahua.

Horse and Pig
Pig allows you free rein so that you won't bolt, but doesn't understand that you like to feel the lash of the riding whip occasionally.

THE HORSE

HORSE AT WORK

You act friendly and uncomplicated in the paddock, but when the race is on, you are out to win, for you are rabidly ambitious. It doesn't matter what race, because you think you can turn your hoof to anything: share dealer in the morning, brain surgeon in the afternoon, burlesque artiste by night. You call it multitasking; we call it "can't hold down a job for longer than it takes to break the photocopier." Although you're ambitious, your hooves don't really work on the corporate ladder, so you have to make an impression in a different way; in movies you are always the maverick cop/doc/quantity surveyor whose bold, unorthodox methods get you the job done, the eye-candy, and your badge back in the last scene. In real life this gets you loathed by less excitable colleagues (Oxen), who have to sort out the paperwork. Always gung-ho to start with, you lose interest rapidly, so if you own a company, it's even money on the staff turning up one morning to find tumbleweed blowing across their desks, and nothing but a hoofprint and a final demand from the electricity company on the floor.

Office Politics

You're great at gossip, sticking your neck out over the gate and letting rip, but politics is all about using information gained in a subtle, restrained, and targeted manner. Sound like you? If you can't unload a secret the minute you hear it (embellished in your own creative style), you explode; and if you don't, rivals always know something's up, for you break out in boils from the stress.

TIME BANDIT	OFFICE INFECTOR	ASSET STRIPPER
As you only have two speeds—workaholic and comatose—and are usually working in the field, how can anyone tell if you are doing the hours?	Why compete when you're off form? And what's wrong with a convincing but unverifiable ailment that recurs when you've got bootleg tickets for the game?	If you use the kit from job A to service job B, hardware from job B to solve glitches in job C, and software from job C to run job A, surely that's good redistribution?

Horse Boss

You love being out in front, so grasp the boss's job without pausing to think whether you can do it. Once in pole position, you stampede the company over the nearest cliff, for your ears are pinned back so hard to your head that you can't hear any advice shouted at you. Your supreme people skill is motivational rhetoric, which means that you exhort your staff to Stakhanovite levels of production on Monday morning … then spend the rest of the week in the bar.

Horse Slacker

You are constantly in motion, so it takes quite a while to work out if you are actually doing anything productive. You only really slack when you're bored—which is quite frequently. If any one of your several jobs gets dull or undemanding, then the devil makes work for idle hooves, and you can't help but liven things up a little by merrily setting fire to the place.

Horse 9–5er

It would be cruel to hobble you this way; if you were an actual horse, The Humane Society would take your employers to court. You can't possibly follow anybody else's schedules, plans, or procedures, and will bolt when unshackled.

Suitable Jobs for Horses

Broncobuster

Televangelist

Circus ringmaster

Timeshare promoter

Mercenary

Roadie

Car thief

HORSE AT HOME

Horse Habitat

Wherever you are, you won't be staying long, so squat or penthouse—it's all the same to you. All you need is an outlet for your cooler (how else will you keep the beer cold?) and running water. Secretly, though, you quite like the idea of a little house on the prairie, as long as you don't have to live in it until you are too old to care, and can just fantasize about it fondly as you hurtle through the starry night on your way to somewhere much more exciting.

Horse Neighbors

Once in your stable, you can't wait to get out to meet the neighbors, wheedling out their secrets, sympathizing with their ailments, their trying days at the office, and their ungrateful lovers. You'll cheerfully lend them cups of sugar or the lawn mower (why not? it's not your sugar or lawn mower), so they don't like to complain about your endless parties, or bottle heaps. Just when they love you like a brother, you move on without returning the $100 they lent you.

Feeding Habits

You'll shovel anything in, any time; because you're constantly on the move, you can't afford to be picky about refueling, and you never know when the next nosebag will come along. You are always the first into the 24/7 fast-food outlet for a pre-dawn double cheeseburger, and you have pizzas-to-go on fast-dial. No host ever feels they've overcatered when you're at the table. All-nite diners, truck stops, and hot-dog vendors worship and adore you.

THE HORSE

Horse Roomie

You love herd life, and housemates love you at first, even if you're flaky with the rent, because you know how to patch into the electrical grid for free, or hook everyone up to unlimited broadband courtesy of next door's wi-fi—plus your parties are legendary. The downside is that you aren't too bothered about whose bed you crash out in; fit in your saxophone practice at 2 a.m.; think that house elves fill the refrigerator and do the chores; and move on without warning or saying goodbye.

Horse Stables

Anywhere roomy and easy to maintain is Horse heaven, and its either got to be mobile or come with enough people already installed to keep you entertained.

* Mack Truck
* Barn (not necessarily converted)
* Montana
* Deep-space freighter
* Backpacker hostel
* Frat house

THE SHEEP

(Also called the Ram and the Goat, as if that's going to fool anybody)

1907, 1919, 1931, 1943, 1955, 1967,
1979, 1991, 2003

FUTURE SHEEP: **2015**

Fixed element:	**Fire**
Energy:	**Yin**
Hour of the Sheep:	**1:00–12:59 p.m.**
Month:	**July**
Season:	**Summer**
Direction:	**South-southwest**
Chinese name:	*Yang*

The Way of the Bleating Sheep

Moody, needy, pessimistic, overemotional, sulky, ingratiating,
theatrical, peevish, fretful, self-pitying, craven, clingy, morbid,
inconsistent, trivial, spiteful, neurotic

Although your fixed element is Fire (*see page 15*), all five Sheep in the 60-year cycle feel unloved and unappreciated in different ways, for each year is ruled by a different element.

Self-indulgent pushover, easily led into Goatish excess; bigger Sheep made you do it—it was not your fault. Lame ducks love you, and you love them, for they make you feel superior.

We say gross extravagance; you say bare necessities, and get testy and ultra-defensive if we point out that one case of Dom Perignon is more than enough for an evening in with the cat.

TEMPERAMENT

In the Western system, we are used to separating sheep from goats: sheep = nice but dim, goats = crafty, slit-eyed, Satan's little cheesemongers. In the Eastern tradition, the Sheep and Goat are considered aspects of the same animal. So, like the Rabbit/Cat (see page 67), you can present as a Sheep (which we are going for), a Ram, or a Goat, but you are actually an unstable combination of all. The Sheep was eighth in the race to Buddha, and eight is the number for prosperity and comfort. Undeserved luck rains down on you, yet you still cower in your field, fretting and moaning and whining and sulking, but refusing to say what your problem is.

We're Poor Little Lambs ...

Despite your Chinese name being *Yang*, you come across as the worst of everything yin: dependent, helpless, frilly, and manipulative. Many male Sheep are not just in touch with their feminine side, but have moved in with it and are arguing about drapes. Sheep with any kind of grip either rebrand themselves as Rams (who'd mess with them horns?) and pretend they come from another part of the zodiac, or exercise the Goat option: still a light-minded mood swinger, but with added recalcitrance and lechery. You can do this because although you come on in public like a poor, wee, hard-done-by wet blanket, your natural element is Fire, the one that signifies initiative, creativity, and

THE SHEEP

WATER SHEEP 1943, 2003

You've heard that the meek will inherit the Earth (you're very impressionable), so you've gone for the Way of Least Resistance and the professional martyr look, to ensure you get your share.

FIRE SHEEP 1907, 1967

The nearest thing there is to an executive Sheep, but the only action is thinking (of the wishful kind ... you could have been a contender) and takes place on Fantasy Island or in your dreams.

METAL SHEEP 1931, 1991

Androids probably dream of you. Your bodywork may be titanium, but your circuitry is Stone Age. You're incompatible with change and, like all mechanical devices, you need constant servicing.

aggressive action. It's just that you express initiative and getting your own way using indirect, but big-gun tactics, such as emotional blackmail (the brimming eye, the trembling lower lip), power sulking, and your favorite: passive aggression.

This contradiction is easier to understand if you remember that in the Western zodiac you inch your way fearfully along the apron strings that attach Smother Mom Cancer to Big Daddy Capricorn, so although driven entirely by emotion, you are shrewd enough to see how far this can get you. And don't think we can't see through the coy, I-cannot-cope-with-the-world schtick. You can't resist grandstanding and love to be pulled blinking into the spotlight, where you stay until they drag you out again. Every Oscar winner who has gone over the top at speech time is a Sheep or has a Sheep scriptwriter.

NOTORIOUS SHEEP

No really, you couldn't possibly … Oh, all right then. Among the parasites and sociopaths, including Jesse James, shot down at home (by a friend he had betrayed) while making esthetic changes on the hang of a picture, look at these two big guns:

Benito Mussolini (b. July 29, 1883)
Power Sheep: he hated the strict rules at his tough school, until his Momma took him out of it. Although anti-Catholic, he sucked up to Pope Pius XI when it suited him, and rode to victory on policies designed to please the rich and powerful. After swapping allegiances like a teen queen (anti-German in WWI, Hitler's best friend in WWII), he invaded France—but only after Germany had done all the work. What he really liked was hearing the crowd roar "Duce! Duce!" because they loved him.

Michelangelo Buonarotti (b. March 6, 1475)
Although a hugely talented artistic superstar (the Sheep's great plus is outstanding artistic genius), M. Buonarotti was withdrawn, touchy, foul-tempered, impossible to work with, hypersensitive to criticism, over-budget, and wrote a self-pitying sonnet about how tough it was painting the Sistine Chapel; even popes and Medici dukes could not deal with him.

Sheep Mantra
I blame you

COMPANION ANIMALS

You also have an animal that sniffs around the hour of your birth (see pages 12–13 for details). According to Chinese tradition, the animal in charge of your birth hour gives you your social mask, the yang self that you present to the world.

The Hour of the Rat

11:00 p.m.–12:59 a.m.
Impresario Rat helps drama queen Sheep to transform bleating self-pity into a paying proposition. Twice-daily performances of *Little Lost Lamb* never fails to pull 'em in.

The Hour of the Snake

9:00–10:59 a.m.
Snake ruthlessly suppresses any weak, woolly Sheep behavior and entices your inner Goat to come out. Getting it back in again is the challenge.

The Hour of the Ox

1:00–2:59 a.m.
You may loathe each other down on the farm, but this combination turns dithering Sheep into authoritative Ram, an iron hoof in a velvet sock.

The Hour of the Dragon

7:00–8:59 a.m.
Dragon feeds Sheep with delusions of grandeur: an avenue of Ram-headed sphinxes now leads to your door.

5:00–6:59 a.m.
Very demure Sheep, instantly lost in the crowd, making it very easy to dodge unnoticed behind the barn when the flock goes to market.

The Hour of the Tiger

3:00–4:59 a.m.
Diva overload as Tiger's volatile, unfocused passion is fueled by Sheep's operatic mood-swinging. Oscars all round.

The Hour of the Rabbit

Your native hour, the Hour of the Sheep, wanders between one and three in the afternoon—just the time for a long, self-indulgent late lunch, or a long, self-indulgent massage. There's little point in going back to the office, is there?

THE SHEEP

The Hour of the Horse

11:00 a.m.–12:59 p.m.
Able to go whole days without bleating, you shop on your own with your own money and hold down a job, for you want a bit of independence. One of the zodiac's few self-funding Sheep.

The Hour of the Pig

9:00–10:59 p.m.
Your outer Pig forces you to feel the pain of others, but your inner Sheep can control Pigs with emotional blackmail, so you demand empathy back, with interest.

The Hour of the Sheep

1:00–2:59 p.m.
Double dosed with clingy fretfulness, you make Blanche DuBois look like Condoleezza Rice. If it wasn't for the kindness of strangers, you'd be stew.

7:00–8:59 p.m.
Rebellious Ram, ready to head-butt anyone, especially the farmer, who disagrees with the way you run this flock.

3:00–4:59 p.m.
Monkey brings out the Goat buried under the Fleece of Discontent, and together you nimble up the mountains.

5:00–6:59 p.m.
Regardless of any actual talent, you come on like a textbook artistic genius, in thrall to your imaginative muse, but unable to change your socks or a light bulb.

The Hour of the Dog

The Hour of the Monkey

The Hour of the Rooster

SHEEP
IN LOVE

*Incurably romantic, adorably
scatterbrained, whimsical, flirty,
and coy—that's you in attack
mode, and it rarely fails. Partners
are besotted for a few heady
weeks, until Love Potion No. 9
wears off, then they stare at you
aghast and realize they will never
get out. There will be pet names;
clingy and possessive is putting it
mildly. You recall every little
anniversary (Our First Pizza),
but sulk for weeks if they don't.
How could they be so cruel to poor
little you? Petulant mood swings,
theatrical sighs, meaningful looks,
sobbing touchingly in public, and
never ever telling your lover what
they have done wrong and how
they can make it better means
that some of the dimmer ones
spend the GDP of small countries
on shiny gifts because they feel
guilty, but don't know why ...*

Sheep in Bed

Once you've maneuvered the love
object between the flowery sheets
(making them think it is all their idea,
in case you want to holler harassment
when you find out they're not rich
enough), you release the inner Goat
(or Ram) and give it everything. After
the first loss-leader, you withhold all
further Goat rides (no one has as many
migraines as you do) until you get what
you want, which is a titanium pre-nup.

Hot Sheep

Unsurprisingly, these are all people who cluster at the Ram's and Goat's end of the pasture, because a full-on Sheep is such hard work that the cutest butt in the world doesn't make it worth it. So how about Mick Jagger, a supreme Goat in every way, Jumpin' Jack Flash in person and still playing the field.

And there's more … High-testosterone Sheep—Mel Gibson, Billy Bob Thornton, John Wayne (yes, really)—operate a modified version of the passive-petulance gambit; the Strong and Silent treatment. It may feel old-school romantic for the first few days, but it's really just armed sulking.

SHEEP DATE

If you find yourself asking a Sheep for a date
without knowing how, that is because Sheep has
put in the hours being ingratiating and flattering.
(Sheep specialize in the ugly or ancient, yet
loaded.) They will be two hours late (they are
so silly about time—they really, really need a new
Rolex), but make up for it by looking blindingly
gorgeous and finding your conversation riveting, so
you forgive them instantly. They can only drink
vintage Champagne, because cheap wine gives
them a headache, and dither delightfully over
the menu until you decide on the most expensive
dish for them. They laugh tinklingly at your jokes,
and after dinner let you lead them past Cartier's,
where they stare hungrily at the window display,
then give a little shrug and sigh and walk on.
Of course they let you pay their cab fare home—
it's the least they could do.

MATING MISTAKES

Sheep and Rat
Sponging charmer meets charming sponge; it will get nasty when you both discover you are penniless gamblers.

Sheep and Ox
Oxen have no time for grasshoppers like you; they know exactly which part of the paddock you come from, and that swinging red light on the gate really annoys them.

Sheep and Tiger
Aren't Sheep the animal of choice to be tethered out by frightened villagers when Tigers are on the rampage?

Sheep and Rabbit
Rabbit doesn't mind indulging you, because you are sitting on a gold mine and they are angling to be Mr. or Ms. 30 percent when the market's right.

Sheep and Dragon
Dragons despise your self-abasement and sentimental sobbing; they've scorched far too many virgins for that old trick to work.

Sheep and Snake
They like to have you around because they adore pretty, complaisant little things, and it's much healthier to keep meat fresh on the hoof.

Sheep and Horse
They were your backup if you didn't get a better offer before your butt sagged, but now they've run away to join the circus.

Sheep and Sheep
The lovers most likely to be found smothered to death under a heap of cuddly toys, scented love notes, heart-shaped candles, and videotapes of *Ghost* and *Love Story*.

Sheep and Monkey
They goad your inner Goat to come out to play, then run away, leaving you to explain to the cops about the pentagram and skulls.

Sheep and Rooster
You recycle the nutrition and exercise programs that Rooster has kindly drawn up for you, and use them as giftwrap, because you don't do dawn or self-discipline.

Sheep and Dog
They cut you out from your girlfriends and herd you into a field you don't like, but fold when you start your bottom-lip wobble.

Sheep and Pig
Whatever you whisper plaintively that you want, Pig will go to the Moon to get it for you; the fun bit is changing your mind two seconds after they have delivered.

SHEEP AT WORK

You have to be bullied into work by people who care enough about you to help you release your inner artiste—it's simply too much for you to do alone. Almost everything (except shopping) is too much for super-sensitive you, which is why everyone else ends up doing your work for you, because they get so irritated (Tiger) or feel sorry for you (Pig). You have to be pushed up the corporate ladder because there is a logjam behind you (you hate change, and your new desk won't be as pretty), and no one can face the tears and tantrums of firing you; a clever manager (Monkey) will move you sideways onto a dear little velvet-covered ladder of your own, which you can go up and down all day without bothering anyone. Actually, you cannot see the point of work, because it never brings in the kind of money that a self-indulgent hedonist like you needs. Luckily, your inner Goat has some kind of psi connection with the cashflow of the cosmos, and so arranges it that aunts you never knew expire and leave you loaded; you win lotteries with a ticket bought by an admirer; or you have to beat off Sugar Daddies or Mommies with a not very big stick.

Office Politics

Evasion, ingratiation, smiling at people you loathe, and blaming everyone else comes naturally to you—as does forming cliques just so that you can freeze people out of them, if they don't pay you enough attention. If anyone takes you on, you bleat piteously and run and hide behind your line manager.

TIME BANDIT	OFFICE INFECTOR	ASSET STRIPPER
You never get in before mid-morning and have to go home early, because crowds bring on the panic attacks, but you always leave for lunch on the button.	Of course you feel fragile most of the time, but always struggle in to work, so that people can see your suffering and feel as sorry for you as you do yourself.	A few minutes' sweet talk to the spotty one in Accounts gets you access to the company credit cards; you charge your cab rides and florists' bills to your boss.

Sheep Boss

Because you cannot make a decision, you dither until someone else makes it for you, then blame them if it goes wrong. However, you are pretty and well mannered, so shadowy figures who for legal reasons cannot actually be named as boss always choose you as easily replaced front person. You don't mind being a powerless figurehead as long as the expense account is good and fat.

Sheep Slacker

They call you the Slackmeister, because you work harder at not working than the rest of us do at working. By the time you have decided what kind of coffee you want, opened your emails and replied to the important personal ones, distracted everyone on a deadline, and wandered around the office currying favor, it's time to go home.

Sheep 9–5er

Secretly, you love being bullied into a routine by masterful Oxen and Dragons. (Did I say you were consistent?) It gives you a fine excuse for discontented whining at the water cooler, tears in the washroom, complaining that you are being picked upon, resentment at how much easier everyone else has it, and making everyone else feel guilty about how down-on-your-luck you are.

Suitable Jobs for Sheep

Hostess

Trophy wife

Princess

Gigolo

Boy toy

PR consultant

Courtesan

SHEEP AT HOME

Sheep Habitat

If you are a prize Sheep, you are sponging it in luxury at someone else's expense or are so rich people fall over themselves to lend you the château. Any property you own was left to you by the grumpy second cousin whom only you bothered to visit in the old folks' home. It may be a downtown basement, but in your head it is a dear little cottage with roses around the door, and you stuff it with tiny objects, for you love trivia and diminished worlds and giving things dinky names.

Sheep Neighbors

As a Sheep, you worry theatrically about the neighbors, as you do about everything. Supposing they are ax murderers? Run a crack den? Don't like your drapes? You dare not confront them—you might find out that they are blameless counter clerks after all and have to find something else to fret about. As a Ram, you patrol the yard borders to make sure they know what's yours. As a Goat, you visit with homemade cookies to see if they have anything you might want.

Feeding Habits

All-day grazing at finger-food buffets is your idea of heaven, which is why you like crashing weddings and bar mitzvahs. Your favorite foods are tiny and fiddly: canapés, petits fours, cocktail wieners, cupcakes, vol-au-vents, mini-muffins … because you can stuff down twice as many without looking greedy. You adore little animals and would love to be vegetarian, but you have no self-control; still, you weep as you scarf up all the oysters.

THE SHEEP

Sheep Roomie

You spend most of your time in your boudoir (from the French *bouder*, to sulk), coming out only to moan about how you can feel every pea under your 12 skimpy mattresses, how everyone else's room is way nicer than yours, and how it could not be your fault the bathtub overflowed again (even though you were in it at the time). You burst into tears when asked to do chores, cajole everyone into paying extra to hire a cleaner, then burst into tears again when asked for your share. You don't pay rent.

Sheep Pens

The smaller and more sweetly pretty, the better—and staff are essential. Sheep are quite happy to stay in any meadow anywhere, as long as it's lush and they're not paying.

* Miniature village
* Little House on the Prairie
* Alpine chalet
* Borrowed petit château
* Dollhouse
* The Best Little Whorehouse in Texas

猴

rHE MONKEY

1908, 1920, 1932, 1944, 1956, 1968,
1980, 1992, 2004

FUTURE MONKEY: **2016**

Fixed element: **Metal**

Energy: **Yang**

Hour of the Monkey: **3:00-4:59 p.m.**

Month: **August**

Season: **Summer**

Direction: **West-southwest**

Chinese name: *Hou*

The Way of the Gibbering Monkey

Superficial, sly, vain, selfish, arrogant, smug, lying, cheating, nosy,
unscrupulous, light-fingered, disrespectful, crafty,
über-competitive, overconfident

Although your fixed element is Metal (*see page 15*), all five Monkeys in the 60-year cycle run different-sized rings around the rest of us, for each year is ruled by a different element.

You can't let it alone, can you? Never satisfied with what you've got, or the state of the world, you are always trying to reinvent the wheel, redraft the laws of gravity, or cut a better deal.

For a Monkey, you are quiet and studious, but that is so you can work your way into a system and destroy it from within; a Nobel or Pulitzer will deflect you, because you love to be appreciated.

TEMPERAMENT

You are the nearest DNA match to humanity on the zodiac and, wouldn't you know it, the most badly behaved. In many Asian traditions you are synonymous with guile, and people try to neutralize you, by making you a god or by learning how to trick you back using your own greed, smug overconfidence, and curiosity to lure you into traps. The Monkey came ninth in the race to Buddha, and nine is that annoying number whose multiples add up to itself in what seems like mystical trickery to non-math majors; an excellent choice for you, because Monkey world is also constructed of multiple variations, but they are all just aspects of you.

Too Much Monkey Business

All hail the zodiac's resident sociopath. You know all the rules, but none of them apply to you because you are too smart, fast, and clever to be hamstrung by regulations, which are only there to give you the edge over plodders like us. As we are all so very dull, you are forced to spend a lot of your time winding us up (especially Tigers, who fall for it every time). So what if anyone calls you out? You are armor-plated in self-belief. Peer approval means nothing to you: you think you are pretty damn fine. In the Western zodiac, you swing nonchalantly on the liana that links Leo to Aquarius, which gives you unshakable self-confidence and great hair, plus a bright, shiny intellect to misuse.

猴 THE MONKEY

WATER MONKEY 1932, 1992	FIRE MONKEY 1956, 2016	METAL MONKEY 1920, 1980
You scratch my back, I'll lacerate yours. You'll collaborate with anyone if the money's right, which is why so many Monkey Air planes loaded with food aid fly right off the radar so often.	Hot-eyed life and soul of the sales conference, a tedious practical joker with grubby, groping fingers. Secret morbid fears that everybody wants to kill you are entirely justified.	Too arrogant to bother disguising your contempt for the rest of us, you perch alone on the top branch of your minimalist tree, dropping coconuts on the heads of anyone who dares touch it.

The Rat thinks you are God (but then so do you, and you *are* in many cultures). Rats do conning; you do Transparent Conning—which is where you con us blind, let us see that you are doing it, we let you know we have seen you doing it, and we still fall for it. Basically you're the bored smart-ass kid in the back row, talking back to teacher, getting cheap laughs from the class, entertaining yourself with jokes and pranks, and messing with stuff. If it ain't broke, you can't wait to fix it, poking and pressing giant red buttons that have a label underneath reading DO NOT PRESS. And how can you do all this with never a twinge of regret or shame? You are a solipsistic fantasist. The world is a construct of your brilliant imagination, so if you break it—while seeing if you can make atoms any smaller, for instance—you can always make another one, can't you?

NOTORIOUS MONKEYS

You don't need a role model for how to behave badly; it's hard-wired into you.
However, you like to do mischief by stealth, so who's to know who you are? Among
the fantasists, philosophers, escapologists, pranksters, and hucksters, think about:

Leonardo da Vinci (b. April 23, 1452)
Renaissance Man's Renaissance Man: artist, sculptor, engineer, anatomist, architect, etc. As soon as he became a genius at one thing, he moved on to another, inventing six inconceivable things before breakfast and writing it all down backward, just because he could. Insatiable curiosity, sea-level boredom threshold, and Addictive Fiddling Disorder, you see. Despite being low-born, he hung out with popes, dukes, and wealthy Florentines, always following the money.

Timothy Leary (b. October 22, 1920)
Smart academic who got fed up with being a dull psych lecturer at Harvard, so he broke the rules, played the system, outwitted the FBI, escaped from prison (leaving a sarcastic note explaining how), famously experimented with LSD (turn on, tune in, drop out), and kept searching for the final frontier of the human mind. His dying words were "Why not?"

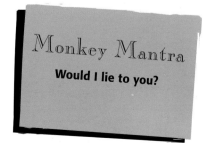

Monkey Mantra
Would I lie to you?

COMPANION ANIMALS

You also have an animal that sniffs around the hour of your birth (see pages 12–13 for details). According to Chinese tradition, the animal in charge of your birth hour gives you your social mask, the yang self that you present to the world.

The Hour of the Rat

The Hour of the Snake

The Hour of the Ox

The Hour of the Dragon

The Hour of the Tiger

The Hour of the Rabbit

11:00 p.m.–12:59 a.m.
Unstoppable combination of wit, guile, and smarts. Not only do you get to have your cake and eat it too, you also know how to burn the candles on top at both ends.

9:00–10:59 a.m.
Terrifying combination of subtle power, wit, and clever fingers means you can get in and out of anywhere unchallenged; a top-class assassin.

1:00–2:59 a.m.
An unimaginative suit; only when people get out of the boardroom and check the small print do they realize how comprehensively they've been had.

7:00–8:59 a.m.
A fatal tendency to think you really are a powerful Monkey god means you start up grandiose schemes you can't finish.

5:00–6:59 a.m.
Rabbit keeps your triumphant gibbering to a minimum, and helps you study body language. Amazed punters think you can read their minds and give you all their money.

3:00–4:59 a.m.
Tigers and Monkeys should keep out of each other's jungles. Self-confidence overload leads to disaster in the end.

Your native hour, the Hour of the Monkey, goes from three until five in the afternoon, when everyone loses a little focus and gets careless about leaving their cellphones and credit cards on the desk when they dash out to get a candy bar.

猴 THE MONKEY

The Hour of the Horse

11:00 a.m.–12:59 p.m.
You get a bit restless hustling all day long, and love playing games, so why not combine both sets of talents and play the games using your new rules, designed to let you win?

The Hour of the Pig

9:00–10:59 p.m.
People are convinced by your honest face, and you really mean to keep your part of the deal, but inner Monkey persuades you to blow the money on fun instead.

The Hour of the Sheep

1:00–2:59 p.m.
Same old scheming and conniving, but drenched in Chanel; it's even more fun convincing saps that giving you the keys to the condo was their idea.

3:00–4:59 p.m.
The world will not survive a double dose of the Monkey's biological imperative to open boxes they shouldn't.

The Hour of the Monkey

7:00–8:59 p.m.
Fewer tricks than other Monkeys, but that's because you worry constantly that they will go wrong and you won't get a reward.

The Hour of the Dog

5:00–6:59 p.m.
You're not too good at keeping all your intricate plots and schemes under wraps, and you can never resist providing a helpful step-by-step how-to manual with every scam.

The Hour of the Rooster

MONKEY IN LOVE

Everything's a game to you, especially love. You quickly learn the rules of engagement so that you know how the rest of us are playing, then you lie, cheat, bluff, distract, deceive—whatever it takes to win. Novelty, mischief, and the chase are what you like best, which is why you target the love of your best friend's life, your more attractive in-laws, career virgins, your boss, and so on. And it's no fun if you're not playing several games at once, like a Grand Master taking on a bunch of doomed chess nerds. You despise anyone who falls for you, and when you have got your clever little hands on someone's heart, there's nothing you like better than to take it to pieces. When you can't find the beat, you just throw it away, because you can easily get a new one.

Monkeys in Bed

You are very hot stuff, but easily bored, so no vanilla sex, unless you haven't done it for years and it has regained novelty value. There is no sexual style, orientation, or fantasy you won't try, and gender-blurring makes things even more fun: dressing up, role play, threesomes, fivesomes, orgies, key parties, s & m, bondage, dogging ... You can't get no satisfaction, nor would want to, because that means you would have to stop.

Hot Monkeys

Donatien Alphonse François, Marquis de Sade (b. 1740): supreme Metal Monkey; perverse, libertine aristocrat who dedicated his life to breaking the rules ("Are not laws dangerous that inhibit the passions?"), even though it meant that he spent a lot of time in the madhouse or behind bars. No sexual experiment was too weird or violent for him, but it was the philosophy behind it all that was his true passion. He wrote it all down, but his son burned most of the manuscripts, so we will never know.

And there's more ... Although the Marquis is hard to beat (ouch!), there are lots of powerful female heartbreakers (Liz Taylor, Jerry Hall, Lisa Marie Presley, Dolly Parton), who don't give a stuff about the rules, so non-Monkey guys are always in danger.

猴 THE MONKEY

MONKEY DATE

Nobody in the history of the universe has ever said
No to a Monkey—and neither will you, even if you
are married with six kids, a recluse, or in traction.
Don't be surprised, when they pick you up in the
stretch limo they have scammed, if you're on a
foursome, which means one Monkey and three
dates. Monkeys love the challenge of sweet-talking
all of you into staying. There is a risk they might
get a bit bored with only one date to bedazzle,
plus they cut a sweet bulk-discount deal with the
restaurant/bar/club. After an evening full of Monkey
talking at you, you are all whisked off to a cool
party, where Monkey has fixed to meet another
four dates, picks up a new little friend from the
crowd, and tries to sell one or more of you to
business associates. You get your own cab home.
Monkey won't call. Would you want them to?

MATING MISTAKES

Monkey and Rat
After the initial blast, the thrill goes out of being a role model; Rat can never quite keep up with your style changes.

Monkey and Ox
Oxen will do anything for you, so you use them to batter down the armored doors of the local bank.

Monkey and Tiger
Tigers are so easy to wind up and get into a fury that you lose interest and baffle them by being sober and rational.

Monkey and Rabbit
Anybody who gets tricksy with you has got to be very smart indeed, but Rabbit makes use of pretending to be helpless—something you've never mastered.

Monkey and Dragon
As you are both gods, you respect the Dragon. Anyway, if things get too hot, you can always scamper higher up the tree to get away from their flame.

Monkey and Snake
Snakes are in it for the long game and know that you get impatient and careless waiting for them to show their hand.

Monkey and Horse
They give a very bracing gallop and you've learned to whisper into their ear in such a way that they will do anything you want.

Monkey and Sheep
You like to run these as a flock, and they don't seem to have any objection, but it's becoming very expensive.

Monkey and Monkey
Attention Deficit heaven as you meet the one who can change direction as quickly as you can; you can play *Liaisons Dangereuses* together, with the rest of the zodiac as your sex toys.

Monkey and Rooster
They squawk at you, you gibber right back and pluck out their feathers. It's a fair fight, but the neighbors call the noise police.

Monkey and Dog
You are the classy acrobatic jewel thief. They are Inspector Plod. This would be quite a good game if they weren't playing for real.

Monkey and Pig
Gullible old Pig believes every word you say, so to get any fun out of it, you make up stupendous Munchausen-sized lies.

THE MONKEY

MONKEY AT WORK

What company wouldn't kill to have a brilliant, sly, unscrupulous cut-throat like you on its books? An endless source of genius scams, you move fast, maneuver punters into happily signing (in their own blood) a deal that pays you to take their every asset, and even before the signature is dry, you have broken the contract and renegotiated a far better one with someone else. Sharp eyes makes sharper practice, you chatter, sailing exhilaratingly close to the wind while speed-reading the paperwork so that you can wrongfoot the enemy. If there is any unpleasantness, you will easily argue it away, because you can find ends to justify any means—as long as you are paid enough. You are ultra-competitive, and will not hesitate to hurl anyone off the corporate ladder if they are in your way, even if it is a family firm and it's your dad blocking the rungway. You can sell anything to anyone, but what you sell best is yourself, to the highest bidder. Loyalty is for Dogs; no one should think they have a Monkey on a chain, and if they paid you an obscenely enormous golden hello, then they are more the fools.

Office Politics

Knowledge is power. By coffee time on your first day you've scanned every databank, got a handle on the current gossip and murky history (you are so easy to talk to), and found out where the bodies are. In the afternoon you are promoted to CEO. If it's been that easy, you might just resign next day. You only came to fix the photocopier.

TIME BANDIT	OFFICE INFECTOR	ASSET STRIPPER
You blur about the place at warp speed, so no one is quite sure if you are in. It's not easy keeping good time doing three jobs in different states, but you manage.	You stagger in on crutches, covered in purulent buboes and dog bites; everybody stampedes, leaving their wallets behind. Oh, what a Merry Prankster you are.	They should never have given you that inch. Now the company assets are signed over to Whole Nine Yards, Inc., and you lease back the real estate at a profit.

Monkey Boss

You'll let them beg you to be boss, and maybe even cut a few killer deals if you are feeling mellow, shut down a couple of low-performance departments, negotiate the workers out of their rights, and so on; but you are only doing it so you can get headhunted by bigger, richer companies. You always make a point of covering your tracks before you move on, and dropping the people who promoted you into deep doo-doo.

Monkey Slacker

Look, the idea is to get a result, right? Does it matter how? You are not about to bore yourself senseless redoing stuff someone else has done, when you could be partying. So you get in early, copy over all their files, wipe their hard drive, and give the presentation as yours. Apparently it's called plagiarism.

Monkey 9–5er

You master any routine task in 15 minutes, finish it in 30, do it all again with one hand, then tinker about with the methodology to make it work faster—and it's still only eleven o'clock. So you start a blackjack school in the washroom, jam the intranet with spam, reroute the pension fund into your own account, and seduce the mailboys. At lunchtime, you cut your losses and leave.

Suitable Jobs for Monkeys

Lawyer

Fraudster

Asset stripper

Forger

Insider trader

Pornographer

Agent (any kind)

MONKEY AT HOME

Monkey Habitat

You like to be up high up above the urban jungle, so you can look down on everyone else and get a good view of what's going on in the world—and how you can use it to your advantage. You live light (always ready for a quick getaway), so go for gadgets rather than furniture, unless it's the inflatable kind, because it's such fun sticking in a pin when pontificating assholes are sitting on it. Wherever you are, you won't be there next week, so the repo men don't bother.

Monkey Neighbors

As soon as you move in, you doorstep the neighbors with a bottle of impressive wine and your most vivacious persona, because you are pathologically nosy, one or more might be worth seducing, and you want to case the joint for valuables. They'll soon invite you for dinner by the pool (you don't have one); their *casa* will be *su casa* (but not the other way around, of course). You'll move on (leaving a false address) before they even miss the Philippe Starck flatware.

Feeding Habits

You go to the best restaurants, where you nimble around the table charming everyone with your amazing closeup magic tricks, to distract them while you nibble away at their gourmet dishes (like Rat, but stylish: more beluga than french fries) and take cheeky little swigs of their Bollinger. Then you kiss hands, make their final coin disappear, and bow out gracefully before the bill arrives; how to have your cake and eat it, Monkey style.

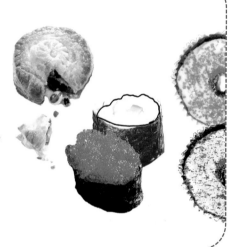

猴 THE MONKEY

Monkey Roomie

You only agree to move in if your one simple rule is followed: you share everyone else's stuff, but they don't touch yours. After a house meeting where you go turbo on the sparkle and charm, everyone agrees that this is only fair and they are lucky to get you. The stories you tell every month about why you can't make the rent are so entertaining that your housemates applaud wildly and pay what you owe themselves, in appreciation of a Master. Chores? Why not—who knows what you'll find?

Monkey Houses

The main thing about a Monkey house is that it must be full of toys, gadgets, and distraction, with plenty of space to party in. For example:

* FAO Schwartz
* Caesar's Palace
* Disneyworld
* Peter Pan's Neverland
* Roof garden
* Coney Island

THE ROOSTER

(Also called the **Hen** and the **Chicken**, which makes you really mad)

1909, 1921, 1933, 1945, 1957, 1969,
1981, 1993, 2005

FUTURE ROOSTER: **2017**

Fixed element: **Metal**

Energy: **Yin**

Hour of the Rooster: **5:00–6:59 p.m.**

Month: **September**

Season: **Fall**

Direction: **West**

Chinese name: *Ji*

The Way of the Squawking Rooster

Self-righteous, nitpicking, bossy, domineering, vain, proud,
rude, tactless, hypercritical, opinionated, abrasive, impatient

IN YOUR ELEMENT

WOOD ROOSTER 1945, 2005　　　**EARTH ROOSTER** 1909, 1969

Although your fixed element is Metal (*see page 15*), all five Roosters in the 60-year cycle crow at slightly different times in the morning, because each year is ruled by a different element.

Attempts at world domination are always scuttled by your fatal urge to complicate and turn a simple battle plan into an academic feasibility study, with footnotes and three appendices.

We have let you down, we have let ourselves down, and now the whole zodiac will have to stay behind, until whoever strung all your paperclips together into a Kabbalah bracelet owns up.

TEMPERAMENT

Some Eastern astrologers downgrade you to Chicken or Hen. Ha! You are taking them to the Zodiac Tribunal, where you will represent yourself, and win, because no one else can argue the opposition into the ground and compost them in backup paperwork like you. Then you can resume your perch on the Moral High Ground and carry on your work as CEO of Barnyard, Inc. You came tenth in the race to Buddha, as planned, because 10 is the perfect number, according to the best authorities (Pythagoras). It had nothing to do with your spending so long preening your tail feathers and buffing your beak that you set off a smidgeon later than scheduled.

Cock-a-doodle-do

You would commit *coq-au-vin* rather than admit it, but those astrologers have a point. Sometimes the Chicken is strong in you: strutty, flamboyant peacock on the outside, quivering heap of clucking anxiety inside. No one could possibly miss you—not with that bright red hat on—but you're still not sure you've been noticed and have to blast us all from sleep to point out your radiant gloriousness. From dawn until dusk you make CSIs look slack as you detail through long, dull tasks in a forensic ecstasy. At night your little head fills with grandiose, ridiculous dreams (you were swapped as an egg and are rightful heir to Colonel Sanders's empire, etc.).

THE ROOSTER

WATER ROOSTER 1933, 1993	FIRE ROOSTER 1957, 2017	METAL ROOSTER 1921, 1981
Thinktank supremo; the system wizard. Your plan to solve the healthcare crisis means that 50 percent of the population has to be terminated, but you cannot fault it as a logical solution.	You burn too intensely for this world, and suffer from delusions of Phoenixhood, even though you know it is illogical to believe that you can be born again from the ashes of your dead self.	Your spurs still gleam, as do your hot, mad little eyes, but you've been unemployable since cockfighting was made illegal, so you spend your time glaring at anybody who invades your space.

In the Western zodiac you peck along the trail of scattered corn that leads detail-fetishist Virgo to weak-willed sensationalist Pisces—a highly organized mess. Your chicken feed is empathy-seed free, so you are always what you call candid (and what we call insensitive). No one is in any doubt about your opinion on any subject, and will be beak-lashed into submission if they disagree. You broadcast criticism as easily as you take outraged offense at any thrown back at you. You don't need anyone's advice (you are perfect), but are happy to hand it out by the bucketload. Beady eyes like yours are great for following an established blueprint, but you can't see over the farm fence to the grand design, so you miss life's big prizes. You're the only zodiac animal with proper wings—so why didn't you fly across the river and get to Buddha first?

NOTORIOUS ROOSTERS

You don't take kindly to suggestions that you are less than unique, but anyone swaggering about in eye-catching, yet strangely conservative finery, perfectionists, medal-heavy generals, and formidable women could be of the same feather.

Richard Wagner (b. May 22, 1813)

Controversial, opinionated, self-regarding composer, who took simple mythic stories (doomed love, lust for gold) and elaborated them into complex works of musical drama stuffed with interweaving details (leitmotivs). Determined to control every aspect of his work, Wagner wrote the libretti, composed the music, conducted the finished works, and even built a *Festpielhaus* in Bayreuth for them to be performed in; never afraid to speak his mind, regardless of the fallout.

Catherine the Great (b. April 21, 1729)

The supreme role model for strong-minded Rooster women everywhere, Catherine married Peter, Grand Duke of Russia, when she was 16. Observing that he was not up to the job on his accession as Peter III in 1762, she had him overthrown, took up the reins of power (if you want a job done well, do it yourself), and gave Russia 30 years of enlightened rule.

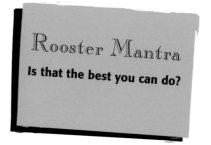

Rooster Mantra

Is that the best you can do?

THE ROOSTER

COMPANION ANIMALS

You also have an animal that sniffs around the hour of your birth (see pages 12–13 for details). According to Chinese tradition, the animal in charge of your birth hour gives you your social mask, the yang self that you present to the world.

The Hour of the Rat

11:00 p.m.–12:59 a.m.
Your outer Rat applies your nitpicking skills to traditional con games so that you can make them even more efficient; you can't resist a complication too far.

The Hour of the Snake

9:00–10:59 a.m.
In ancient Greece, and still in Africa, the Rooster is an oracular being that pecks out prophecies using seeds set next to to mystic symbols. You are that Rooster.

The Hour of the Ox

1:00–2:59 a.m.
General George Patton (a fellow Rooster) driving a Sherman tank into the enemy with all klaxons turned up to 11 would be a pussycat compared to you.

The Hour of the Dragon

7:00–8:59 a.m.
Implacable: you will nuke your own farmyard, and die with an ironic smile on your beak rather than cede a scrap of authority.

5:00–6:59 a.m.
Roosters and Rabbits don't match, but when Rabbit turns off your squawk-box and rebrands you as Chicken, you find that you get fatter worms and a lot more seed.

The Hour of the Tiger

3:00–4:59 a.m.
With Tiger in command, you may as well be a headless Chicken; you know how to rush about, but not how to function.

The Hour of the Rabbit

Your native hour, the Hour of the Rooster, fits neatly into the early evening hours of five until seven, the time for most people to leave the office and Rooster to have a last look around to check that all the desks are tidy and the lights are turned off.

 THE ROOSTER

The Hour of the Horse

11:00 a.m.–12:59 p.m.
Horse likes a flutter, but on a reasonably sure thing, so stops you putting all your tail feathers on a colorful, blind, three-legged outsider because you dreamed it romped home.

The Hour of the Pig

9:00–10:59 p.m.
Mother Hen who insists that everyone drinks your Chicken soup (no sacrifice is too great) and snuggles under your wing at 8:00 precisely every night.

The Hour of the Sheep

1:00–2:59 p.m.
Hen—and proud of it. It's warm and dry, you get fed, you can gossip with the flock., and your chicks get taken off to nursery before they get bothersome.

The Hour of the Dog

7:00–8:59 p.m.
Excellent. Barking is almost as effective as crowing, and Dog likes to patrol electrified perimeter fences in uniform as much as you do.

5:00–6:59 p.m.
Double Rooster. Factory robots need counseling after you have savaged their working practices and standards of efficiency. You found the Marine Corps too lax.

The Hour of the Monkey

3:00–4:59 p.m.
Very cocky, crafty Rooster, you cut a deal with the fox (fewer raids in return for regular birds in the hand), so you can have more fun.

The Hour of the Rooster

ROOSTER IN LOVE

When one half of a couple says, "We need to talk," you know it's as good as over, just as it is when celebs renew their marriage vows. It's like that from day one with you. Roosters can't wait to talk, from that very first soul-melting kiss (are you sure you flossed today, dearest?). You squawk budding relationships out of existence, criticizing the love object's wardrobe, opinions, musical taste, and bed prowess—not only does size matter, you'll get out your digital tape measure and prove it. To make up for this carping overload, you are unable to express loving feelings (they're safely caged up in your heart), and refuse to whisper sweet nothings as they are illogical. So lovers dump you, even though you look good, and you spend the next couple of years overanalyzing why.

Rooster in Bed

Rooster males swagger, hinting that the little red rooster is always too lazy to crow by day, owing to being down and dirty all night long. This is boasting. When you do get between the sheets (you iron them first, of course), you always follow a similar vigorous routine program, with plenty of shouting. Hens expect regular attention, and will flap off to a new roost if it's not delivered.

Hot Roosters

Swashbuckling is a secondary sex characteristic with Roosters, and lots of slightly old-fashioned professional Hollywood "hellraisers" are/were Roosters. However, D. H. Lawrence wins on all-round Roosterishness: he not only gave forensic accounts of sexual intercourse, but also liked to strut about Bloomsbury salons being blunt, earthy, and hypercritical, yet ran away to Mexico when his own work was slated.

And there's more ... Fascinating Rooster women who are/were not prepared to put up with nonsense, and who make strong men thrill with the idea of being dominated, include Yoko Ono, Joan Collins, Bette Midler, Joan Rivers, Deborah Harry, and Michelle Pfeiffer.

鷄 THE ROOSTER

ROOSTER DATE

Feel flattered, or possibly stalked—a Rooster date is not a random flight of fancy. There will have been planning, a selection process you didn't even know about, a credit check. Rooster will arrive glossy and groomed, and it is not a good idea to outlabel them. Neither is it a good idea to suggest where to go or what to do, but you know this, because Rooster has already emailed and txtd the evening's itinerary and timetable to you, and backed it up with a message on your voicemail. Don't express any strong opinions, and do NOT be late. Roosters wear everything on their sleeves except their hearts, so won't tell you how ardently they love and admire you, although they will tell you that your shoes are scuffed and your pimple cream isn't working. Whether you like it or not, Roosters always call: your number is now on weekly redial in their Blackberry.

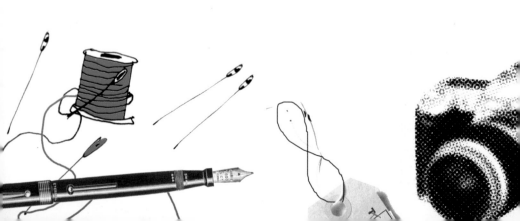

MATING MISTAKES

Rooster and Rat

You may be be a sucker for flattery and fawnication, but even you know that what Rat really wants is access to the hen coop.

Rooster and Ox

This one won't fly. You have never dated, and you won't ever, because neither of you will agree to the other one's schedule.

Rooster and Tiger

By the time you've proofread Tiger's ardent love poems, they will be writing sonnets to someone else's beautiful plumage.

Rooster and Rabbit

They find your entire wardrobe an embarrassment; it doesn't help that you spend most of the time you are together rubbing Rabbit's fur up the wrong way.

Rooster and Dragon

You promise Dragon all the treasure they can eat, just to keep them down on the farm, but then can't deliver, so you get your feathers singed as they flap out of your life.

Rooster and Snake

You're mesmerized, but can't be bothered with hot, slow passion at strange times in the afternoon when you should be chairing the interdepartmental data-merging symposium.

Rooster and Horse

It annoys you intensely that Horse can win races without listening to any of your stride-by-stride advice on how to do it properly.

Rooster and Sheep

Put away that Salvation Army bonnet. When are you going to learn that Sheep do not want to be saved from themselves?

Rooster and Monkey

You pride yourself on putting all your cards on the table; of course Monkey can't resist palming the ace, then hiding it up your own sleeve to make you look foolish.

Rooster and Rooster

What fool of a chicken farmer puts two Roosters in one yard? Now you know why cockfighting was a blood sport. Even brightsiders say this is a cosmic no-no.

Rooster and Dog

Unlikely: Dog is always the banner carrier in any street protest, and you're always the arresting officer when the riot kicks off.

Rooster and Pig

Pig takes you out for a good time at their favorite diner, and you take the opportunity to critique their table manners, dress code, and lack of portion control.

ROOSTER AT WORK

Your unique blend of OCD nitpicking and impossible dreams probably functions best in the military (or anywhere you can get a glamorous uniform and can do strutting, with medals); actually, you are most likely to die under friendly fire, because your constant punishment detail has driven your troops over the edge. You are relentless, perfection is the goal, and you are the only one who reaches it; being only human is not an option. You work hard, but always peck off more than you can chew, never let anyone help, and then fall at the last fence. Anyone who dares mention this pattern gets their eyes pecked out. Your strategy of choice is complication. Show you a big, simple idea, and you nag it to shreds so that you can deal with them one at a time; the job is never-ending and you get to bustle about self-importantly forever.

It's called Mission Creep. Myopic attention to detail means that you get stuck on the lower rungs of the corporate ladder, too busy analyzing the wood grain to move on up; it also explains why you can never see a hostile takeover coming, but go ballistic if your desk is moved slightly to the left.

Office Politics

You only ever go to the water cooler if you want a drink, and to reprimand slackers who spend too much time there. You never listen to gossip, and say exactly what you think. So you are chickenfeed for the zodiac's Machiavellis (Rabbit, Snake, Monkey), who can get you stuffed and oven-ready in less time than it it takes to boil an egg.

TIME BANDIT	OFFICE INFECTOR	ASSET STRIPPER
Unofficial Chronological Law Enforcer; you never waste company time, and set up time-and-motion studies so no one else in the workforce can, either.	The crow must go on … You never miss a day, even if you are sick, and always self-medicate. This explains why everyone else is off right now with bird flu.	Management puts you in charge of all assets, certain you will set up an ironclad system that makes requisitioning a new pencil so soul-destroying no one will try.

Rooster Boss

Are you not first in any pecking order by your very nature? You are the terror of the boardroom, scrutinizing every bottom line, micromanaging the company into the ground, and browbeating everyone into toeing your line. The company goes down the drain, because lateral thinking has no place on any agenda of yours, and you don't move with the times because underneath the sharp suits and theatrical ranting you are an old-school conservative.

Rooster Slacker

You would not know how—unless the grandiose dreamer who lives deep in your head escaped from the coop, then you could waste hours planning the design details of your unbuildable opera house. It's also hard to disconnect you from the Internet, an endless system of infinite undifferentiated detail. Bliss!

Rooster 9–5er

Now you're talking … Routine you can do. The more Hennish of you love playing Chicken Licken, bustling about doing everything yourself, asking others to help for form's sake, but flapping on before they can say Yes or No. (You'd be stuffed if they said Yes.) At the end of the day you are exhausted, but you get to feel smug, self-righteous, and indispensable—just like you wanted.

Suitable Jobs for Roosters

Supernanny

IRS inspector

Personal trainer

Critic

Drill sergeant

CSI chief

Grand inquisitor

Cult deprogrammer

ROOSTER AT HOME

Rooster Habitat

Wherever you are, you act as if you own the place, so we can never be sure where you live, but a giveaway would be overkill in the walk-in clothes closet and filing cabinet department. And the self-portraits. Decor is either hyper-ornate or edgily eccentric: chicken wire and adobe walls teamed with Tiffany chandeliers; you let us think this is stylishness, but it is just tightwad Rooster going eyeball-to-eyeball with spendaholic Rooster for control of the budget.

Rooster Neighbors

Fortunately for your neighbors, you are out most of the time, patrolling the farmyard to give the flock their daily fix of your utter brilliance and authority. Otherwise you are constantly on the doorstep/phone/email with candid comments on their general slobbiness and lots of helpful advice about how they can bring themselves up to your standard. If they don't come up to scratch within 24 hours, you go in with your SWAT team. You are only doing your duty.

Feeding Habits

You eat out regularly at your usual table (the one where everyone can see you). You won't enjoy yourself unless you've made a few cutting remarks about fork placement and told the chef how to improve his signature dish, but the clever maître d' distracts you with a cocktail that the mixologist has invented especially for you: complicated layers of bright, sticky liqueurs, 10 types of garnish, and real umbrellas, served in a glass bucket.

Rooster Roomie

It was all so disorganized when you first strutted in, but after three or four late-night house meetings (with nibbles), everyone finally saw things your way, mainly because they had a 12-hour shift in ER the next day. Now daily chore lists are mailed directly to everybody's cellphones, CCTV covers the refrigerator to catch Rat red-pawed, there is a timelock on the bathroom, and the cookie jar is electronically tagged. You're never late with your rent unless Versace are having a sale.

Rooster Coops

The ideal Rooster roost should be grand and flamboyant in scale and/or decor, yet have a complicated inner infrastructure for Roosters to organize. How about:

* Neuschwanstein (Ludwig II of Bavaria's fantasy palace)
* Broadway Theater
* Empire State Building
* Westpoint
* Chartres Cathedral
* Guggenheim Bilbao

THE DOG

1910, 1922, 1934, 1946, 1958, 1970,
1982, 1994, 2006

FUTURE DOG: **2018**

Fixed element: **Metal**

Energy: **Yang**

Hour of the Dog: **7:00–8:59 a.m.**

Month: **October**

Season: **Fall**

Direction: **West-northeast**

Chinese name: *Gou*

The Way of the Howling Dog

Defensive, angst-ridden, cynical, pessimistic, contemptuous,
fault-finding, stubborn, judgmental, self-important, argumentative,
cantankerous, impatient

Although your fixed element is Metal (*see page 15*), all five dogs in the 60-year cycle cock a leg at the fire hydrant in different ways, because each year is ruled by a different element.

WOOD DOG 1934, 1994

You ain't nuttin' but a hound dog, and you ain't doing nuttin' without the rest of the gang, so you don't do anything except mill around in circles or patrol the streets looking for other packs.

EARTH DOG 1958, 2018

Hardbitten, world-weary, cynical, and yet wearily upright, like Philip Marlow, except when you are hardbitten, world-weary, cynical, and sleazily downright, like a crime baron or a serial killer.

TEMPERAMENT

East or West, Dogs make the rest of us nervous, either because you are the zodiac's cops and we know we must be guilty of something, so you may turn on us rabidly any minute, or because all that unconditional loyalty makes us feel nauseated; or perhaps it's the dogged determination to be our best friend, even if we've already got best friends. You came eleventh in the race to Buddha; you must have been hanging back to keep us under surveillance (a good cop keeps all suspects in full view, and Pig is your deputy). Numerologists say that 11 is a Master Number; on the darkside, it represents treachery and betrayal. No wonder you're suspicious.

A Dog's Life

Oh dear! It's all black and white to you—but mostly black, because the name on your dog tag is Gloombucket. The world is a dreadful place (it would help if you took off your dark glasses), you know badness and doom are out there, and it's your job to sniff them out and lay them at our feet. It's always a sad day for you if there is a horrific air crash and everyone survives; little Timmy is rescued alive and happy from the well; or the rains come and save the harvest—because it means fewer things for you to feel bad about. You flagellate yourself daily, allegedly because you cannot cure all the world's ills (you are, after all, just one small mutt), but really, deep down, because you enjoy it.

犬 THE DOG

WATER DOG 1922, 1982

One of the sleeping dogs who should be let lie; a veteran member of the elite ROBT (rolling over and being tickled) team, you are routinely assigned to sleep in front of the fire.

FIRE DOG 1946, 2006

Leader of the pack. A rebel with a cause—first to the barricades, a firebrand clenched between your fierce teeth because you really hope your followers will beg you to set fire to yourself.

METAL DOG 1910, 1970

When they cry havoc and let slip the dogs of war, they mean you, the relentless, fanatical Iron Dog, who takes no prisoners and obliterates enemies. Few want to take you on a walk.

Your martyr gene means that you're always willing to take the bullet. We daren't think what you want in exchange, but suspect it's satisfaction of your constant, craven, crowd-pleasing urge for approval. Just because your own self-esteem runs at low pressure, it doesn't stop you counseling everyone else (especially when they don't ask), because you know best and can pinpoint all the bad things they're doing.

Although never actually happy, you are deeply miserable if you don't have a Cause or Mission; once the stick has been thrown, you're after it like a shot, but if several are thrown at once, you get confused and sink into directionless gloom. In the Western zodiac you follow the scent between Libra and Aries, at once raring to go and waiting to see what the options are: a dithering warrior, like Hamlet, the Great Dane (oh, please).

NOTORIOUS DOGS

It's scary the number of violent gangsters, murderers, and mass murderers in your kennel, not to mention US presidents; just for once, I think you need to see an upside: saints, freedom fighters, and Judge Dredd. Otherwise, it's the following.

Charles Manson (b. November 12, 1934) Born No-Name Maddox and abandoned by his mother, Manson started stealing before he hit teendom and was in and out of jail for minor crimes (pimping, driving stolen cars, passing stolen checks), all aggravated by him busting parole or crossing state lines. When he came out of San Quentin in the Summer of Love (1967), he created his own darkside "family," a pack of disaffected young people who took murderous revenge on society; he's been locked up since 1971.

Al "Scarface" Capone (b. January 17, 1899)

What is Gangster No. 1 if not leader of the pack? In 1920s gangland, Capone was Chicago's vicious top dog, the FBI's most-wanted: drugs, liquor, protection rackets, gambling, homicide, the St. Valentine's Day Massacre (allegedly), etc.; brought down by the IRS in the end (aren't we all?). A very bad Dog indeed. You should all be perversely proud.

Dog Mantra

Expect the worst

K THE DOG

COMPANION ANIMALS

You also have an animal that sniffs around the hour of your birth (see pages 12–13 for details). According to Chinese tradition, the animal in charge of your birth hour gives you your social mask, the yang self that you present to the world.

The Hour of the Rat

The Hour of the Snake

The Hour of the Ox

The Hour of the Dragon

The Hour of the Tiger

The Hour of the Rabbit

11:00 p.m.–12:59 a.m.
Rent-a-moralist; you have found a way to turn high ideals into hard cash and are now a much-loved pundit on Oprah and have set up your own chain of charity stores.

9:00–10:59 a.m.
They call you Cerberus, after the three-headed, snake-tailed hound of Hades, but not to your face of course. If we want to live, we call you Mr. Cerberus.

1:00–2:59 a.m.
Bulldog, of course; once you've got something or someone between your teeth, you never let go, not even for lunch or comfort breaks.

7:00–8:59 a.m.
You scour the country looking for people to rescue. If you can't find any, you set fire to a few towns to create demand.

5:00–6:59 a.m.
You would never commit to one master, because you never know who is going to come along with a tastier brand of doggy treat, a bigger basket, or a classier stick to throw.

3:00–4:59 a.m.
Passionate, impatient, and always agitating for reform, even when it has just been instituted after your last effort.

Your native hour, the Hour of the Dog, covers the early evening watch from seven until nine. It's the end of another hard day and either dark or, worse, dusk—the kind of light in which you can't tell friend from foe, so better assume the worst.

The Hour of the Horse

The Hour of the Pig

The Hour of the Sheep

The Hour of the Dog

The Hour of the Monkey

The Hour of the Rooster

11:00 a.m.–12:59 p.m.
Your act is the Adorable Trail Mutt who can't bear a collar, but stays as long as the widow/orphan/drunk needs you; amazingly, this always coincides exactly with the minute you get bored.

9:00–10:59 p.m.
You like to keep a keg of five-star Cognac on the collar in case you're unexpectedly sent to rescue frostbitten mountaineers. So what if you live in Oklahoma?

1:00–2:59 p.m.
Your outer Sheep wants a life of gross indulgence on silk cushions with candy bones, but your inner Dog keeps rounding you up and sending you to boot camp.

7:00–8:59 p.m.
Your outer Dog is freedom fighting in Nepal while your inner Dog runs workshops on Marxist theory for the puppies.

5:00–6:59 p.m.
High moral tone modulated through insatiable curiosity, fanatical attention to detail, and the urge to wear red; it's a shame that the Spanish Inquisition is no longer recruiting.

3:00–4:59 p.m.
Dear little doggy who can beg, bark out the answers to hard sums, shake paws, walk on hind legs, and pick pockets.

DOG
IN LOVE

God, you are such hard work! Defensive and suspicious, you sidle into every relationship crippled with doubt and anxiety, and usually snapping and biting to drive the love object away, because you cannot stand the strain of waiting for it all to end in tears. Nothing will ever convince you that your true love really, really loves you, so you Woody Allen away, interrogating the relationship rather than living it; of course they dump you. Or you go for the Fido option, sitting at home with ears pricked, ready to hurl yourself at them, drooling with needy affection; so they stop coming home. You don't help yourself by incessant fault-finding and acid remarks about their moral turpitude—no, they won't thank you in the end; they'll leave.

Dog in Bed

You're already anxious enough, because you know you shouldn't really be on the bed at all, plus you're listening for break-ins. Your favorite part is afterward, when you get to ask your lover if your performance was up to snuff, and then ask them again, until they're forced to shut you up by reading aloud from the Thomas Hardy novels you keep at the bedside to get you in the mood.

Hot Dog

Think about it: Hound Dog? Suspicious Minds? Jailhouse Rock? Love Me Tender? Surely Elvis was the hottest of Dogs himself (as well as eating them by the truckload)? Especially when he was gorgeous, young, pouting, leather-pants, pelvis-swiveling Elvis. Adored by most of the planet, yet never convinced of it, the King was happiest roaming around with a gang of hangers-on.

And there's more … Consider the gorgeous Dogs who constantly reinvent themselves so that we will all love them (Cher, Madonna) and those irresistible hobo Dogs who don't take kindly to the leash (Bill Clinton).

人 THE DOG

DOG DATE

You probably accepted this date because Dog
stared at you with big, sad eyes, or lay at your feet
until you said yes. (Warning: wolves in Dog suits
use this maneuver to get a mercy shag.) Don't
expect a high-maintenance evening, for Dogs don't
approve of luxury and will expect you to walk or jog
to the meeting point, where they will be an hour
early, so that they can work themselves up into a
lather of anxiety expecting you not to show. You'll
start at the consciousness-raising meeting they are
facilitating, then go on to the soup kitchen where
they help out. If it's raining, you patrol the wet
sidewalks together, as Dog asks you which way you
vote and tells you the relationship just isn't working
and maybe you should both get counseling. If you
get to a second date, you may end up at their
place, but only to help get the banners ready
for tomorrow's protest.

MATING MISTAKES

Dog and Rat
Rat can easily rewire a lie detector, but won't get past your dawn interrogation about where they have been all night and why they are wearing someone else's pants.

Dog and Ox
Imagine a passionate affair between Adolf Hitler and Che Guevara. You can't, can you? Or maybe you can.

Dog and Tiger
You met on the barricades and their passion and commitment to the struggle blew you away, but when you called around with background literature, they'd left home.

Dog and Rabbit
They do politics, you do Causes; they had you fooled until the day they brought your lunch to the picket line in their Porsche.

Dog and Dragon
Although you wave the constitution in their face, Dragon ignores all basic democratic processes; they never offer to consult before dragging you out to the Ritz.

Dog and Snake
You are thrilled because you think you have converted an aristocrat; Snake just fancies a bit of blue-collar rough.

Dog and Horse
You gallop along happily for a few miles until you realize that they have longer legs and it won't occur to them to wait for you.

Dog and Sheep
You've put way too many Sheep away on indecency charges to be tempted, although the urge to round one up and reform them is sometimes irresistible.

Dog and Monkey
Irreproachable community leader falls for irresistible swindler; and somehow you've signed away the rights to Monkey TV's mini-series of the whole sordid affair.

Dog and Rooster
Rooster wants to reform you, but that is your job. It all ends in tears when they make you upgrade your wardrobe and wear a collar.

Dog and Dog
Neither of you trusts the other one; you both think you've fallen in love with the counselor who facilitates your relationship, and now need anger management help.

Dog and Pig
Pig indulges your every whim and agrees with all your cogently worded arguments; they must be pulling the old honey trap.

DOG AT WORK

Your trouble is you resent working for the man, but you have to serve somebody, even if it does mean doing ludicrous tricks some of the time. Probably this is why you are cranky, critical, difficult to work with, and always suspicious if the boss class offers a tempting pay package. Seek the Hidden Agenda is your favorite game. Clever managers use you to test-run new business ideas, because you will immediately sniff out everything that could possibly go wrong with them, saving the company megabucks in consultancy fees. And because you are a plain speaker and can't see the point in putting off bad news, you are the one ordered to announce layoffs, downsizing, etc. in your bluntest possible way, so that Rabbit can swan in afterward and play good cop. You like to think you have no time for the corporate ladder, as you are strictly commune, but can't resist barging into meetings uninvited and offering advice to the CEO, even if you have refused all promotion and still work the elevator. Your inner Fido wants to be rewarded with their approval, and you are ashamed of yourself.

Office Politics

No one is left in any doubt about your real-life politics, but you despise office games. That's okay, for no one dares play them with you; you are tactless, judgmental, snappy, bark out any sensitive information you're given, never switch allegiances because you prefer martyrdom, and can turn ferocious without warning. Monkey thinks you must have a double-bluff secret agenda. You don't.

TIME BANDIT	OFFICE INFECTOR	ASSET STRIPPER
Even if you are a very bad Dog indeed, you put in the hours and then some; you're on duty 24/7, so you can feel satisfyingly contemptuous of the rest of us.	You always soldier on, but quickly get sent home, for most people are uneasy around a Dog with red eyes and a lot of saliva, even if you insist it's only a cold.	You use the photocopier to run fliers advertising Justice for Krill's next protest. Come the revolution, you will be first in there with an ax to smash the entire IT system.

Dog Boss

Although you are happy to be leader of the pack, as long as the pack agrees, you are thrown into total anxiety meltdown as non-elected master. Defeatist and pessimistic, you see pitfalls at every turn, and if they're not there, you'll create them. You're hopeless at shareholder meetings, where you tell it like it is and watch the stock plummet. Your Pig PA fondly thinks that because you are cantankerous and gloomy, you must have a heart of gold.

Dog Slacker

No dog is a slacker, although you tend to fall to pieces in front of a roaring fire or on hot sidewalks. However, you don't do dissembling, so if there is nothing to do, you don't do it. Despite being at constant mental attention, you lack the sense to look busy. Promotion goes to Rat, even though you do their shifts.

Dog 9–5er

You start out a loyal pack member, keen to obey orders. It does not take you long to nose out that your line manager is on the take, Rabbit and Monkey are running their own business in company time, and Rat is selling the office furniture on eBay. You blow the whistle and are instantly fired. Great! Fighting an unfair dismissal case is your idea of heaven.

Suitable Jobs for Dogs

Union leader

Police chief

Saint

Freedom fighter

Gang leader

Martyr

DOG AT HOME

Dog Habitat

Unless you've sold out and gone lapdog, you would rather share a drafty kennel with comrades than a gilded palace with a tool of Wall Street. An ex-army tent will do you, or a kibbutz; a squat is even better, for you can challenge the fascist hegemony of the propertied class and have somewhere to put your Che and Anti-Globalization posters at the same time. All you really need is a large security blanket, a good fire, and a handmade string leash to show that you belong.

Dog Neighbors

It's more than likely that the neighbors are cons on the run, undercover hit persons, or worse; you patch into police radio to check for any APBs out on them, log their car registration, and note down patterns of behavior, just in case it all goes off. You've never let them past your own front door, but you visited them the day they moved in, to scope the place for anything suspicious and to let your inner collie sniff out whether they were sheep, goats, or the CIA spying on you.

Feeding Habits

It's only in cartoons that you are obsessed with sausages. You avoid meat, to show solidarity with fellow creatures, and because you are always worried that your food has been poisoned—either by malign agribusiness or political enemies—you impose strict dietary rules on yourself and anyone within 100 yards. You'll only eat out if it's a sustenance lunch with fat-free vegan cheese and tap water, but can't resist a donut on a stakeout.

Dog Roomie

You love house-sharing: it gives you access to a whole new bunch of possible converts to the Cause, and you get to chair communal meetings where a complex process of transferable votes decides whose turn it is to do what. You always do your own chores, confront anyone who doesn't pull their weight (Sheep), and are the self-appointed rent-hound. As the only responsible one, you triple-lock the door at night and Dragon has to break it down to get back in.

Dog Kennels

Because Dogs like to live free and yet communally, but worry endlessly about security, the ideal Dog safehouse must be spacious and well guarded or have the safety-in-numbers factor.

* National Mall, Washington, D.C.
* Woodstock
* Gated community
* Precinct House
* Barrack room
* Rebel stronghold

THE PIG

(Also called the **Boar**, as if that fools anybody)

1911, 1923, 1935, 1947, 1959, 1971,
1983, 1995, 2007

FUTURE PIG: **2019**

Fixed element: **Water**

Energy: **Yin**

Hour of the Pig: **9:00–10:59 a.m.**

Month: **November**

Season: **Winter**

Direction: **North-Northwest**

Chinese name: *Zhu*

The Way of the Wallowing Pig

Credulous, gullible, willful, obstinate, complaisant, fatalistic, indulgent,
defensive, overcautious, naive, condescending, unrestrained,
passive-aggressive, debauched

IN YOUR ELEMENT

Although your fixed element is Water (*see page 15*), all five pigs in the 60-year cycle roll around in mud of a slightly different texture, for each year is ruled by a different element.

WOOD PIG 1935, 1995

Seduced by the mud-side, you love to hang around with the bad guys at the wrong end of the farmyard, and are surprised when they stick you with the stolen piece and the body.

EARTH PIG 1959, 2019

Sheer willpower mounted on sturdy trotters, you take on the toughest jobs without complaint; are you sure you don't have a halo-shaped birthmark or a plain (but magic) sword at the sty?

You are sometimes known as the Boar, but it's hardly an improvement, is it? You may pack protective tusks and look meaner and bristlier, but you are still hunted down and eaten by Medieval Reenactment Societies. Better stick to Pig, and cheer yourself up with the thought that in the East you are loved and worshiped (although you know, deep down, that's because you are going to be center-table at feast time). You came last in the race to Buddha; not because you are bone idle, but because you don't do competitive and you wanted to see what it was all about before committing. It could have been a trap; most things are, you've found.

This Little Piggy

Besides, although you know Buddha would not eat pork, you suspect you were intended as the barbecue for the farewell picnic. There is much sadness in the life of a Pig. By day you are all jovial and life-and-soul, just like it says on the tin, but at night, in the darkest corner of the sty, you wrestle with despair. You know you were born to be somebody else's dinner, so you've decided that as you can't take it with you when you go, you'll have it all now, thank you.

In the Western zodiac you snuffle along the unlikely bond that ties stubborn, stuff-loving Taurus to scary, control-merchant Scorpio. The folksy perception of you is of a naive, gullible, greedy innocent, the preferred

THE PIG

WATER PIG 1923, 1983

Other people's dirty, dark desires are obvious to you, because they're the same as yours; you may reveal all—unless they can help you fund some of your more expensive indulgences.

FIRE PIG 1947, 2007

Intrepid hothead, leader of the slaughterhouse breakouts and cross-state chases that make the news every August, but always caught in the local bar with your head in a bucket of hard cider.

METAL PIG 1911, 1971

Don't overestimate your powers and come on all pigheaded just because you're tough and bristly. A determined charcutier can always roast you as you stand in your oven-ready armor.

mark of every grifter in the zodiac. You know this, so you go into every encounter looking clueless, giving Rat and the others enough rope to hang themselves, while your inner Pig is truffling about decoding the scam. The big downside is your appalling timing. There is always that split second between seeing the need for action and acting, when you catch yourself wondering if, in the light of the karmic wheel—what goes around, comes around—you can be bothered? So you get shafted anyway, even though you saw it coming.

Some of you decide to stick with what you know best—gross indulgence—and hurl yourselves into depravity. The deep impact sends mud spatters to the moon, and pretty soon you look like Jabba the Hutt on steroids, your Bolivian supply lines can't keep up with demand, and the Betty Ford clinic opens a branch in your very own sty.

NOTORIOUS PIGS

There don't seem to be that many Really Bad Pigs, but don't start congratulating yourselves. It's probably because you are too busy spooning chocolate over each other to put yourselves forward; there is always Henry Kissinger, and these two.

Henry VIII (b. June 28, 1491)

One of the few kings of England (1509–47) with an international profile, notorious for excessing all areas: food, drink, wives, fights with the Pope, and for having his own way—all made possible by piles of money left by his Ox daddy, Henry VII. An early supporter of the Greed is Good tendency, Henry VIII's unstoppable greed for a son and heir led to serial wife murdering and seizing religious authority from the Pope. Henry probably died of syphilis. Awesome Piggery.

Oliver Cromwell (b. April 25, 1599)

And at the other end of the forest we have O. Cromwell, Puritan soldier and statesman, inventor of the rigidly moral New Model Army. Cromwell tried really hard to keep his inner hedonist, and everybody else's, under control, with some success; he refused the crown, preferring to be known as the Protector. Pigs always want to be everybody's mom.

Pig Mantra

Enjoy your meal

COMPANION ANIMALS

You also have an animal that sniffs around the hour of your birth (see pages 12–13 for details). According to Chinese tradition, the animal in charge of your birth hour gives you your social mask, the yang self that you present to the world.

The Hour of the Rat

11:00 p.m.–12:59 a.m.
You are the little Piggy that takes himself/herself to market, sucks up to the auctioneer, and makes sure that not all the bacon profits go into the farmer's pocket.

The Hour of the Snake

9:00–10:59 a.m.
Snakes immobilize Pigs, so your inner Pig is trapped and helpless, and you are not the innocent touch you appear to be. Snake loves to double bluff.

The Hour of the Ox

1:00–2:59 a.m.
The three little Piggies built their houses of straw, wood, and bricks; you are the fourth little Pig whose house is built of reinforced concrete and steel.

The Hour of the Tiger

3:00–4:59 a.m.
Wild Boar who prefers liberty and grubbing for acorns in the forest to a safe sty and a full trough on the farm.

The Hour of the Rabbit

5:00–6:59 a.m.
Refined Pig, who likes to spend a lot of time at A-list parties, a glass of the finest wine in the trotter, being obliging and chivalrous, but only to people who really matter.

The Hour of the Dragon

7:00–8:59 a.m.
Roaring Boar, impatient to lead Pigkind to glory, even if the rest of you prefer to stay home and play with the piglets.

Your native hour, the Hour of the Pig, rolls in at the end of the day, from nine until eleven, because you don't like putting yourself forward. Time to veg out, eat a TV supper, have a little nightcap, followed by another little nightcap, then bed.

THE PIG

The Hour of the Horse

The Hour of the Pig

The Hour of the Sheep

11:00 a.m.–12:59 p.m.
Lean, slippery Pig, unusually full of self-esteem; too much of a thoroughbred to be turned into pork products, so you run over the hills and far away if anyone mentions the word knife.

9:00–10:59 p.m.
No one can see what a solid gold beast you are under all that mud and grunting, which is how you like it, or they would tear you to pieces for their share.

1:00–2:59 p.m.
Sentimental Sugar Pig, oppressively overgenerous because you want to buy some time to put off the dreadful moment when you are to be eaten at the feast.

7:00–8:59 p.m.
You are doomed of course, but fight to the death when they come for you, and take as many of them with you as you can.

5:00–6:59 p.m.
Eccentric, theatrical, flamboyant Pig (Ham?), greedy for the limelight and the roar of the crowd; always wants to play Prince Charming, never Baron Blackheart.

3:00–4:59 p.m.
Monkey saves you from being scammed by Rat, but your inner Pig won't let you set up killer scams of your own.

The Hour of the Dog

The Hour of the Monkey

The Hour of the Rooster

PIG
IN LOVE

You are a marshmallow in the fires of love; and knowing you're always going to be hurt, lied to, cheated on, and betrayed doesn't make it any easier. Worshipping from afar is your safest option. Everyone knows when you are in love (which is often) because your heart throbs painfully on your sleeve. You just don't know what to do about it, other than run away or stand perfectly still and wait for the love object to notice you. You hope this will encourage the good guys, but it's the devious bastards who like a challenge and think you are playing hard to get who flock around. When they succeed, you go all obvious and doormatty on them, baking cakes, fixing the house, never complaining, making yourself agreeable and so easy to deceive that they feel duty-bound to do so.

Pig in Bed

You've got buckets of energy and stamina, and grunting, squealing, and rolling around on squashy bits comes naturally to you. So passionate, filthy, do-it-in-the road sex is one of the things you're really good at, as long as love has nothing to do with it. Bonk-buddies who turn up with a magnum of Krug, a crate of raspberries, and a can of whip cream are onto a sure thing.

Hot Pigs

How hot can a Pig get before they are technically bacon? Well, what you lack in looks (let's not lie to ourselves) you make up for in appetite and action, and there are few hotter than Jerry Lee Lewis (the Louisiana Killer, the hard-drinkin', hard-lovin', passionate muthahumpah (his own word) brought low by the scandal that erupted when the media found out his new bride was his 13-year-old second cousin. Well, too much love does drive a man insane. Great Balls of Fire indeed!

And there's more ... The downside of Pig-glorious sex is a tendency to talk about it endlessly afterward—isn't that so, Ernest Hemingway—or even before, Woody Allen.

豬 THE PIG

PIG DATE

It may take a while for you to realize that Pig wants to ask you for a date, because their idea of a pickup line is to get between you and the light and stare dumbly at the wall behind you; or (the other classic Pig move) to walk out of the room the second you walk in. If you are up for it, you can save days of useful time simply by asking them yourself; or, better, sending an email so that their defensive reflexes don't refuse for them, before they can say yes. They loosen up at the restaurant and encourage you to talk about yourself (how winning) because they want to see exactly how you are going to break their heart; they don't talk about themselves—why give you the ammunition? They won't call, but they will want you to; if you get to the third date, book a week's leave, because Pigs are very reluctant to get out of a steaming bed.

MATING MISTAKES

Pig and Rat

You always fall for Rats; for you the thrill is finding out exactly which way they will stitch you up this time. Bigamy, maybe?

Pig and Ox

Maybe Ox doesn't play away, but then Ox doesn't play much anywhere and locks your wine cellar before leaving for work. It doesn't matter, for Rat will let you in.

Pig and Tiger

Tigers may be tempted, but cannot stay, because the mud sticks between their claws and makes it difficult for them to bounce.

Pig and Rabbit

You like being suckered by Rabbit more than anyone else in the zodiac, because at least they know what kind of truffles you like.

Pig and Dragon

A great love match. You stand far away and stare at Dragon because you think they are spectacularly wonderful; they simply don't notice you. This one could last forever.

Pig and Snake

This combination is fatal; even brightsiders say so. Other signs may cheat on you, and batter your heart, but Snakes just can't resist eating you alive really slowly.

Pig and Horse

You put all your money on Horse, but are not entirely surprised when they gallop off into the distance with it.

Pig and Sheep

Sheep makes you feel strong, competent, and in control—just as you secretly think you are; it takes you ages to work out that this is just another method of deceit.

Pig and Monkey

You wait patiently for Monkey to take advantage, but they don't; neither of you realizes that you activate the reflex override that stops them from eating their own young.

Pig and Rooster

Rooster fusses around cleaning up after you've cleaned up, then asks you if you have ironed that shirt. Who needs the stress?

Pig and Dog

You can do without stern lectures on self-discipline, pantry audits, and constant reminders that people are starving somewhere in the world where you aren't.

Pig and Pig

Doomed. You will indulge yourselves to stupefaction, then lay in bed in fatalistic despair waiting for the slaughterhouse van.

THE PIG

PIG AT WORK

You're not scared of hard work—but only when you need the money; it is so much better on vacation. Plus, at an intuitive level, you know the karmic deal the cosmos cut with you: you have agreed to be the feast beast, the Celestial Loser; it's up to the rest of the zodiac to fatten you up, find you work, and make money and other good things flow your way. And they do. So although you are a financial disaster zone, you never hit Skid Row and there's always someone willing to fund your luxury yacht habit. You are a nightmare for methodical colleagues to work with because you fear meticulous schedules (the gods will destroy overconfident planners who usurp the divine prerogative), always cheerfully promise more than you can deliver, and have never knowingly hit a deadline. If confronted about any of this, you grunt churlishly, then retire to the back of your sty and stand in the dark. You don't do competitive; you prefer to usher other people up the corporate ladder ahead of you, because you don't want status (it attracts snipers)—just reward. You prefer a more horizontal approach, involving quite a lot of lying down.

Office Politics

You love clustering around the water cooler for a laugh with all your colleagues, and because you are Captain Affable, everybody thinks you are on their side. You're not; you just know they will all try to use you, but you don't know how. You either wriggle out of any political mess or sit on your butt firmly in one place until it's safe to move, or they send in the cranes.

TIME BANDIT	OFFICE INFECTOR	ASSET STRIPPER
You loathe confrontation, so passive-aggressive tardiness is one of your few weapons. You fit the hours in at times that are inconvenient for everyone else.	If you take sick leave, Monkey will hack into your hard drive and steal all your contracts, so you swig half a gallon of virile flu remedy and arrive just in time.	You don't do it yourself, but Rat and Monkey know how to make it look as if you do. Accounts are always squawking about big bills for phone calls you never made.

Pig Boss

You can do matriarchal: homemade brownies, everyone telling you their troubles, bandaids for grazed knees in the safe, etc., or Boarish, in which case you grunt about in your office, never come out, and everyone trembles at your name. You are hopeless at the confrontation and cut-and-thrust of high-level management (no Pig appreciates the sight of whirling blades), and are quite relieved when the Board stages a managerial buyout, and pays you off.

Pig Slacker

Once and for all, you are not lazy. Making bacon is hard work. You just like to do things slowly, savor the moment, go back and make those tiny adjustments that transform an acceptable meal into a feast. People can either have it good, or on time—but not both. And it is precisely when you are just staring at the wall with your eyes closed, snuffling, that inspiration is upon you.

Pig 9–5er

You put in the hours, but don't like to be bored, so spend most of the time planning the office Christmas party and summer outing, organizing leaving collections and baby showers, and creating an in-house birthday calendar.

Suitable Jobs for Pigs

Human sacrifice

Conflict resolution advisor

Esthete

Mud wrestler

Food taster

Sleep researcher

PIG AT HOME

Pig Habitat

There is a system, based on unstructured heaps and floor visibility, but if you die, no one will know what it is. Brightsiders maintain many Pigs are pristine, but that just means their heaps are cleaner than yours. You focus on essentials: giant tub, industrial refrigerator, chef-standard cooker, comfortable beds, hammock in the yard. Thanks to your bacteria collection, you have an immune system second to none, and dust doesn't get any deeper after three years anyway.

Pig Neighbors

Neighbors love to come around whenever it suits them because they can look at the state your house is in and go home feeling superior about their own; when they get used to it, they stay for coffee (you're not insulted that they bring their own cups—less dishwashing for you) and pour out all their woes, because every Pig functions as the local Emotional Toxic Waste Disposal Unit. It's all part of your karmic destiny, but sometimes you wish they would call ahead.

Feeding Habits

You're not greedy, you just like food, but it has to be good stuff—no blind gobbling of lard or dried cereal in the wee hours. You get very anxious if pantry stocks sink below the minimum requirement for a small town in a nuclear winter, because you like to share and always overcater. You hate wasting food, because you can't bear to think of pheasants, salmon, or even zucchini dying in vain, so you store it all in your love handles and butt cheeks.

THE PIG

Pig Roomie

Housemates love it when you move in, because it's so easy to sucker you into doing all the chores, putting the utility bills in your name, picking up the groceries on your lunch hour as everyone else has mislaid their wallet, and cooking dinner. Everyone complains that you hog the hot tub, even though you brought it with you, so you shower at a friend's. Rat soon learns that you won't ever say no, and drinks all your cooking wine, then borrows your last $5, so that you can't pay your rent.

Pig Pens

The Pig residence must be comfortable, have room for all your mates to sit down for a meal, but a dark corner for you to despair in, and a guaranteed food supply. How about:

* The Rainbow Room
* Dean & Deluca
* Turkish baths
* Nebraska
* Napa Valley

BEAST MEETS WEST

The Western zodiac is ruled by the Sun, and the Eastern by the Moon, so they rarely meet. In fact, until Chinese astrology got a grip on the West a few decades ago, they never spoke. But the Sun and Moon spin around the same sky, so maybe it is worth seeing what kind of bad influence the Western version can have on the East. As this is a book about Chinese astrology, we're not dwelling on the Western version, just giving you a taster. The tables on the following pages show how your year beast expresses itself through the distorting lens of your sun sign.

You will have noted that in each section you've been told that the animal in question paces the line that links two sun signs—for example, Rat skips along between Sagittarius and Gemini. In each case the two sun signs are polar signs: on the zodiac wheel they stand opposite each other and hurl abuse; however, they have certain shamefully shared characteristics, and this is what the Chinese animal sniffs out. We've marked the polar signs for each animal on the tables that follow with a ✳ symbol, so that you won't forget.

Also, because of the season that it is assigned to (see *Animal of the Month on page 11*), each animal has an affinity with the Western sun sign that covers that particular season; so if you are a Rat, for example, tune into Sagittarian horoscopes—even if you are Pisces.

BEAST-MEETS-WEST CHART

RAT

Aries Rat
Charming, ruthless, dominant Rat

Taurus Rat
Foul-tempered, paranoid Rat

Gemini Rat ✳
Motor-mouth, scatterbrained Rat

Cancer Rat
Insecure, paw-wringing Rat

Leo Rat
Pushy, demanding, daring Rat

Virgo Rat
Nosy, intrusive, indiscreet Rat

Libra Rat
Oleaginous, smooth-operator Rat

Scorpio Rat
Intense, addictive, obsessed Rat

Sagittarius Rat ✳
Slippery, sleek, hunch-driven Rat

Capricorn Rat
Severe, status-obsessed Rat

Aquarius Rat
Rebellious, versatile lab Rat

Pisces Rat
Devious, bogusly charitable Rat

OX

Aries Ox
Relentless, executive Ox

Taurus Ox
Immobile, pontificating Ox

Gemini Ox
Shrewd, calculating, deceitful Ox

Cancer Ox ✳
Diehard, mother-knows-best Ox

Leo Ox
Pompous, intimidating, bossy Ox

Virgo Ox
Fussy, ponderous, food-faddist Ox

Libra Ox
Intransigent, butterfly Ox

Scorpio Ox
Power-hungry, self-destructive Ox

Sagittarius Ox
Restless, impatient Ox

Capricorn Ox ✳
Spartan, inflexible, self-righteous Ox

Aquarius Ox
Unpredictable, nonconformist Ox

Pisces Ox
Inconstant, nebulous Ox

TIGER

Aries Tiger
Extra-insanely impetuous Tiger

Taurus Tiger
Obstinate, cage-loving Tiger

Gemini Tiger
Hyperactive, itchy-pawed Tiger

Cancer Tiger
Moody, unconvincing Tiger

Leo Tiger ☀
Sulky, fierce, super-arrogant Tiger

Virgo Tiger
Housebroken, reactionary Tiger

Libra Tiger
Tame, intermittently flashy Tiger

Scorpio Tiger
Ferocious, unfathomable Tiger

Sagittarius Tiger
Pushy, paw-in-mouth Tiger

Capricorn Tiger
Unsociable, conservative Tiger

Aquarius Tiger ☀
Provocative, uncontainable Tiger

Pisces Rat
Soft-centered, temperamental Tiger

RABBIT

Aries Rabbit
Insatiable, lust-driven Rabbit

Taurus Rabbit
Snobby, money-fixated Rabbit

Gemini Rabbit
Dirt-dishing, know-it-all Rabbit

Cancer Rabbit
Self-pitying, brooding Rabbit

Leo Rabbit
Royalty-in-exile Rabbit

Virgo Rabbit ☀
Exacting, hypochondriac Rabbit

Libra Rabbit
Appeasing, compromising Rabbit

Scorpio Rabbit
Recalcitrant, secretive Rabbit

Sagittarius Rabbit
Wild, bold, calculating Rabbit

Capricorn Rabbit
Resolute, non-negotiable Rabbit

Aquarius Rabbit
Feverish, unhinged Rabbit

Pisces Rabbit ☀
Narcissistic, spineless Rabbit

DRAGON

Aries Dragon ☀
Explosive, arrogant party Dragon

Taurus Dragon
Slow-moving, dimly lit Dragon

Gemini Dragon
Slapdash, airhead Dragon

Cancer Dragon
Soppy, sentimental Dragon

Leo Dragon
Imperious, idle, patronizing Dragon

Virgo Dragon
Zealous, unforgiving Dragon

Libra Dragon ☀
Superficial, celeb-collecting Dragon

Scorpio Dragon
Belligerent, cunning, psycho Dragon

Sagittarius Dragon
Undiscerning, naive Dragon

Capricorn Dragon
Solitary, workaholic Dragon

Aquarius Dragon
Mythical, unrealistic Dragon

Pisces Dragon
Make-believe, low-wattage Dragon

SNAKE

Aries Snake
Lethal, risk-taking, outlaw Snake

Taurus Snake ☀
Class-A substance-abusing Snake

Gemini Snake
Devious, slippery, slothful Snake

Cancer Snake
Defensive, style-fascist Snake

Leo Snake
Spoiled, selfish, conceited Snake

Virgo Snake
Cold, autocratic, cutting Snake

Libra Snake
Lascivious, indolent Snake

Scorpio Snake ☀
Venomous, libidinous, killer Snake

Sagittarius Snake
Self-satisfied, uncommitted Snake

Capricorn Snake
Haughty, long-game-playing Snake

Aquarius Snake
Esoteric, contradictory Snake

Pisces Rat
Silent, deadly, blame-shifting Snake

HORSE

Aries Horse
Spendthrift, fickle, fidgety Horse

Taurus Horse
Stable, censorious Horse

Gemini Horse ✴
Shallow-minded, immature Horse

Cancer Horse
Moody, fretful, nervy Horse

Leo Horse
Impatient, vain, overbearing Horse

Virgo Horse
Predictable, highly strung Horse

Libra Horse
Glib, unpredictable circus Horse

Scorpio Horse
Mysterious, rogue, dark Horse

Sagittarius Horse ✴
Fevered, unstable, disruptive Horse

Capricorn Horse
Tethered, austere Horse

Aquarius Horse
Capricious, jaunty, eccentric Horse

Pisces Rat
Suggestible, fantasy-prone Horse

SHEEP

Aries Sheep
Behind-the-scenes fixer Sheep

Taurus Sheep
Idle, luxury-dependent Sheep

Gemini Sheep
Indolent, dilettante, gigolo Sheep

Cancer Sheep ✴
Supine, finicky Sheep

Leo Sheep
Obscenely opulent, diva Sheep

Virgo Sheep
Preachy, priggish, carping Sheep

Libra Sheep
Tetchy, attention-seeking Sheep

Scorpio Sheep
Iron-willed, tough-minded Sheep

Sagittarius Sheep
Upfront, tactless, lusty Sheep

Capricorn Sheep ✴
Mean-spirited, miserly Sheep

Aquarius Sheep
Paradoxical, headstrong Sheep

Pisces Rat
Submissive, maudlin Sheep

MONKEY

Aries Monkey
Vociferous, ADHD Monkey

Taurus Monkey
Clumsy, conflicted Monkey

Gemini Monkey
Indiscreet, game-playing Monkey

Cancer Monkey
Modest, money-magnet Monkey

Leo Monkey ✳
Larger-than-life, hell-raising Monkey

Virgo Monkey
Contemptuous, critical Monkey

Libra Monkey
Cajoling, double-bluffing Monkey

Scorpio Monkey
Lying, cheating, criminal Monkey

Sagittarius Monkey
Erratic, mad-scientist Monkey

Capricorn Monkey
Diligent, money-laundering Monkey

Aquarius Monkey ✳
Mad, bad, dangerous Monkey

Pisces Monkey
Cool, furtive, unreliable Monkey

ROOSTER

Aries Rooster
Brash, loud, rude Rooster

Taurus Rooster
Bellowing, intransigent Rooster

Gemini Rooster
Bossy, laser-tongued Rooster

Cancer Rooster
Indefatigable, nannying Rooster

Leo Rooster
Flashy, lavish, show-off Rooster

Virgo Rooster ✳
Sententious, know-it-all Rooster

Libra Rooster
Languid, chattering Rooster

Scorpio Rooster
Abrupt, high-strength Rooster

Sagittarius Rooster
Slapdash, hyperactive Rooster

Capricorn Rooster
Unflappable, unapologetic Rooster

Aquarius Rooster
Outlandish, controversial Rooster

Pisces Rooster ✳
Dreamy, mood-swinging Rooster

DOG

Aries Dog ☀
Relentlessly keen, hunting Dog

Taurus Dog
Stubborn, dogged Dog

Gemini Dog
Inconstant, straying Dog

Cancer Dog
Needy, insecure Dog

Leo Dog
King/Queen-for-a-day Dog

Virgo Dog
Serious, servile, straitlaced Dog

Libra Dog ☀
Disgruntled, co-dependent Dog

Scorpio Dog
Fanatical, aggressive, willful Dog

Sagittarius Dog
Sniffing, tracking, hounding Dog

Capricorn Dog
Prudish, brusque, sarcastic Dog

Aquarius Dog
Absent-minded, crusading Dog

Pisces Dog
Cringing, defensive Dog

PIG

Aries Pig
Procrastinating, passionate Pig

Taurus Pig ☀
Gross, sybaritic, hedonist Pig

Gemini Pig
Superficial, looks-obsessed Pig

Cancer Pig
Wasteful, dissipated, greedy Pig

Leo Pig
Luxury-loving, self-indulgent Pig

Virgo Pig
Interfering, bad-tempered Pig

Libra Pig
Vacillating, self-absorbed Pig

Scorpio Pig ☀
Vengeful, libertine Pig

Sagittarius Pig
Coarse, thick-skinned, caustic Pig

Capricorn Pig
Possessive, self-disciplined Pig

Aquarius Pig
Defiant, destructive, loner Pig

Pisces Pig
Overindulgent, chaotic Pig

CHINESE CALENDAR YEAR CHARTS

YEAR	FROM	TO	ANIMAL SIGN	ELEMENT	ENERGY
1900	31 Jan 1900 – 18 Feb 1901	Rat	Metal	+ Yang
1901	19 Feb 1901 – 7 Feb 1902	Ox	Metal	- Yin
1902	8 Feb 1902 – 28 Jan 1903	Tiger	Water	+ Yang
1903	29 Jan 1903 – 15 Feb 1904	Rabbit	Water	- Yin
1904	16 Feb 1904 – 3 Feb 1905	Dragon	Wood	+ Yang
1905	4 Feb 1905 – 24 Jan 1906	Snake	Wood	- Yin
1906	25 Jan 1906 – 12 Feb 1907	Horse	Fire	+ Yang
1907	13 Feb 1907 – 1 Feb 1908	Sheep	Fire	- Yin
1908	2 Feb 1908 – 21 Jan 1909	Monkey	Earth	+ Yang
1909	22 Jan 1909 – 9 Feb 1910	Rooster	Earth	- Yin
1910	10 Feb 1910 – 29 Jan 1911	Dog	Metal	+ Yang
1911	30 Jan 1911 – 17 Feb 1912	Pig	Metal	- Yin
1912	18 Feb 1912 – 5 Feb 1913	Rat	Water	+ Yang
1913	6 Feb 1913 – 25 Jan 1914	Ox	Water	- Yin
1914	26 Jan 1914 – 13 Feb 1915	Tiger	Wood	+ Yang
1915	14 Feb 1915 – 2 Feb 1916	Rabbit	Wood	- Yin
1916	3 Feb 1916 – 22 Jan 1917	Dragon	Fire	+ Yang
1917	23 Jan 1917 – 10 Feb 1918	Snake	Fire	- Yin
1918	11 Feb 1918 – 31 Jan 1919	Horse	Earth	+ Yang
1919	1 Feb 1919 – 19 Feb 1920	Sheep	Earth	- Yin
1920	20 Feb 1920 – 7 Feb 1921	Monkey	Metal	+ Yang
1921	8 Feb 1921 – 27 Jan 1922	Rooster	Metal	- Yin
1922	28 Jan 1922 – 15 Feb 1923	Dog	Water	+ Yang
1923	16 Feb 1923 – 4 Feb 1924	Pig	Water	- Yin
1924	5 Feb 1924 – 24 Jan 1925	Rat	Wood	+ Yang
1925	25 Jan 1925 – 12 Feb 1926	Ox	Wood	- Yin
1926	13 Feb 1926 – 1 Feb 1927	Tiger	Fire	+ Yang
1927	2 Feb 1927 – 22 Jan 1928	Rabbit	Fire	- Yin
1928	23 Jan 1928 – 9 Feb 1929	Dragon	Earth	+ Yang

YEAR	FROM — TO		ANIMAL SIGN	ELEMENT	ENERGY
1929	10 Feb 1929 — 29 Jan 1930		Snake	Earth	- Yin
1930	30 Jan 1930 — 16 Feb 1931		Horse	Metal	+ Yang
1931	17 Feb 1931 — 5 Feb 1932		Sheep	Metal	- Yin
1932	6 Feb 1932 — 25 Jan 1933		Monkey	Water	+ Yang
1933	26 Jan 1933 — 13 Feb 1934		Rooster	Water	- Yin
1934	14 Feb 1934 — 3 Feb 1935		Dog	Wood	+ Yang
1935	4 Feb 1935 — 23 Jan 1936		Pig	Wood	- Yin
1936	24 Jan 1936 — 10 Feb 1937		Rat	Fire	+ Yang
1937	11 Feb 1937 — 30 Jan 1938		Ox	Fire	- Yin
1938	31 Jan 1938 — 18 Feb 1939		Tiger	Earth	+ Yang
1939	19 Feb 1939 — 7 Feb 1940		Rabbit	Earth	- Yin
1940	8 Feb 1940 — 26 Jan 1941		Dragon	Metal	+ Yang
1941	27 Jan 1941 — 14 Feb 1942		Snake	Metal	- Yin
1942	15 Feb 1942 — 4 Feb 1943		Horse	Water	+ Yang
1943	5 Feb 1943 — 24 Jan 1944		Sheep	Water	- Yin
1944	25 Jan 1944 — 12 Feb 1945		Monkey	Wood	+ Yang
1945	13 Feb 1945 — 1 Feb 1946		Rooster	Wood	- Yin
1946	2 Feb 1946 — 21 Jan 1947		Dog	Fire	+ Yang
1947	22 Jan 1947 — 9 Feb 1948		Pig	Fire	- Yin
1948	10 Feb 1948 — 28 Jan 1949		Rat	Earth	+ Yang
1949	29 Jan 1949 — 16 Feb 1950		Ox	Earth	- Yin
1950	17 Feb 1950 — 5 Feb 1951		Tiger	Metal	+ Yang
1951	6 Feb 1951 — 26 Jan 1952		Rabbit	Metal	- Yin
1952	27 Jan 1952 — 13 Feb 1953		Dragon	Water	+ Yang
1953	14 Feb 1953 — 2 Feb 1954		Snake	Water	- Yin
1954	3 Feb 1954 — 23 Jan 1955		Horse	Wood	+ Yang
1955	24 Jan 1955 — 11 Feb 1956		Sheep	Wood	- Yin
1956	12 Feb 1956 — 30 Jan 1957		Monkey	Fire	+ Yang
1957	31 Jan 1957 — 17 Feb 1958		Rooster	Fire	- Yin
1958	18 Feb 1958 — 7 Feb 1959		Dog	Earth	+ Yang
1959	8 Feb 1959 — 27 Jan 1960		Pig	Earth	- Yin

YEAR	FROM – TO	ANIMAL SIGN	ELEMENT	ENERGY
1960	28 Jan 1960 – 14 Feb 1961	Rat	Metal	+ Yang
1961	15 Feb 1961 – 4 Feb 1962	Ox	Metal	- Yin
1962	5 Feb 1962 – 24 Jan 1963	Tiger	Water	+ Yang
1963	25 Jan 1963 – 12 Feb 1964	Rabbit	Water	- Yin
1964	13 Feb 1964 – 1 Feb 1965	Dragon	Wood	+ Yang
1965	2 Feb 1965 – 20 Jan 1966	Snake	Wood	- Yin
1966	21 Jan 1966 – 8 Feb 1967	Horse	Fire	+ Yang
1967	9 Feb 1967 – 29 Jan 1968	Sheep	Fire	- Yin
1968	30 Jan 1968 – 16 Feb 1969	Monkey	Earth	+ Yang
1969	17 Feb 1969 – 5 Feb 1970	Rooster	Earth	- Yin
1970	6 Feb 1970 – 26 Jan 1971	Dog	Metal	+ Yang
1971	27 Jan 1971 – 15 Jan 1972	Pig	Metal	- Yin
1972	16 Jan 1972 – 2 Feb 1973	Rat	Water	+ Yang
1973	3 Feb 1973 – 22 Jan 1974	Ox	Water	- Yin
1974	23 Jan 1974 – 10 Feb 1975	Tiger	Wood	+ Yang
1975	11 Feb 1975 – 30 Jan 1976	Rabbit	Wood	- Yin
1976	31 Jan 1976 – 17 Feb 1977	Dragon	Fire	+ Yang
1977	18 Feb 1977 – 6 Feb 1978	Snake	Fire	- Yin
1978	7 Feb 1978 – 27 Jan 1979	Horse	Earth	+ Yang
1979	28 Jan 1979 – 15 Feb 1980	Sheep	Earth	- Yin
1980	16 Feb 1980 – 4 Feb 1981	Monkey	Metal	+ Yang
1981	5 Feb 1981 – 24 Jan 1982	Rooster	Metal	- Yin
1982	25 Jan 1982 – 12 Feb 1983	Dog	Water	+ Yang
1983	13 Feb 1983 – 1 Feb 1984	Pig	Water	- Yin
1984	2 Feb 1984 – 19 Feb 1985	Rat	Wood	+ Yang
1985	20 Feb 1985 – 8 Feb 1986	Ox	Wood	- Yin
1986	9 Feb 1986 – 28 Jan 1987	Tiger	Fire	+ Yang
1987	29 Jan 1987 – 16 Feb 1988	Rabbit	Fire	- Yin
1988	17 Feb 1988 – 5 Feb 1989	Dragon	Earth	+ Yang
1989	6 Feb 1989 – 26 Jan 1990	Snake	Earth	- Yin

YEAR	FROM	TO	ANIMAL SIGN	ELEMENT	ENERGY
1990	27 Jan 1990 – 14 Feb 1991		Horse	Metal	+ Yang
1991	15 Feb 1991 – 3 Feb 1992		Sheep	Metal	- Yin
1992	4 Feb 1992 – 22 Jan 1993		Monkey	Water	+ Yang
1993	23 Jan 1993 – 9 Feb 1994		Rooster	Water	- Yin
1994	10 Feb 1994 – 30 Jan 1995		Dog	Wood	+ Yang
1995	31 Jan 1995 – 18 Feb 1996		Pig	Wood	- Yin
1996	19 Feb 1996 – 7 Feb 1997		Rat	Fire	+ Yang
1997	8 Feb 1997 – 27 Jan 1998		Ox	Fire	- Yin
1998	28 Jan 1998 – 15 Feb 1999		Tiger	Earth	+ Yang
1999	16 Feb 1999 – 4 Feb 2000		Rabbit	Earth	- Yin
2000	5 Feb 2000 – 23 Jan 2001		Dragon	Metal	+ Yang
2001	24 Jan 2001 – 11 Feb 2002		Snake	Metal	- Yin
2002	12 Feb 2002 – 31 Jan 2003		Horse	Water	+ Yang
2003	1 Feb 2003 – 21 Jan 2004		Sheep	Water	- Yin
2004	22 Jan 2004 – 8 Feb 2005		Monkey	Wood	+ Yang
2005	9 Feb 2005 – 28 Jan 2006		Rooster	Wood	- Yin
2006	29 Jan 2006 – 17 Feb 2007		Dog	Fire	+ Yang
2007	18 Feb 2007 – 6 Feb 2008		Pig	Fire	- Yin
2008	7 Feb 2008 – 25 Jan 2009		Rat	Earth	+ Yang
2009	26 Jan 2009 – 13 Feb 2010		Ox	Earth	- Yin
2010	14 Feb 2010 – 2 Feb 2011		Tiger	Metal	+ Yang
2011	3 Feb 2011 – 22 Jan 2012		Rabbit	Metal	- Yin
2012	23 Jan 2012 – 9 Feb 2013		Dragon	Water	+ Yang
2013	10 Feb 2013 – 30 Jan 2014		Snake	Water	- Yin
2014	31 Jan 2014 – 18 Feb 2015		Horse	Wood	+ Yang
2015	19 Feb 2015 – 7 Feb 2016		Sheep	Wood	- Yin
2016	8 Feb 2016 – 27 Jan 2017		Monkey	Fire	+ Yang
2017	28 Jan 2017 – 15 Feb 2018		Rooster	Fire	- Yin
2018	16 Feb 2018 – 4 Feb 2019		Dog	Earth	+ Yang
2019	5 Feb 2019 – 24 Jan 2020		Pig	Earth	- Yin

INDEX

Picture credits

The author and publishers are grateful to the following for permission to reproduce illustrations: The Art Archive: p.199; The Art Archive/Culver Pictures: p.107; The Art Archive/Galleria degli Uffizi Florence/Dagli Orti: p.151; The Art Archive/Fondation Thiers Paris/Dagli Orti: p.43; The Art Archive/Marc Charmet: p.135; Bettmann/CORBIS: pp.23, 39, 71, 87, 103, 119, 167, 183, 203; Bridgeman Art Library: p.155; Hulton-Deutsch Collection/CORBIS: p.171; The Kobal Collection: pp.75, 123; Paramount/The Kobal Collection: pp.91, 187; Selznick/MGM/The Kobal Collection: p.27; 20th Century Fox/The Kobal Collection/Morton, Merrick: p.59; Warner Bros/The Kobal Collection: p.55; Warner/Goodtimes/The Kobal Collection: p.139.